WADSWORTH Pi

ON

JAMES

Robert B. Talisse
Vanderbilt University

D. Micah Hester
Mercer University School of Medicine

Australia • Canada • Mexico • Singapore • Spain • United Kingdom • United States

Printed in Canada
1 2 3 4 5 6 7 07 06 05 04 03

Printer: Transcontinental-Louiseville

ISBN: 0-534-58397-0

For more information about our products, contact us at:
Thomson Learning Academic Resource Center
1-800-423-0563

For permission to use material from this text, contact us by:
Phone: 1-800-730-2214
Fax: 1-800-730-2215
Web: www.thomsonrights.com

For more information contact:
Wadsworth-Thomson Learning
10 Davis Drive
Belmont, CA 94002-3098
USA

Asia
Thomson Learning
5 Shenton Way #01-01
UIC Building
Singapore 068808

Australia/New Zealand
Thomson Learning
102 Dodds Street
Southbank, Victoria 3006
Australia

Canada
Nelson
1120 Birchmount Road
Toronto, Ontario M1K 5G4
Canada

Europe/Middle East/South Africa
Thomson Learning
High Holborn House
50-51 Bedford Row
London WC1R 4LR
United Kingdom

Latin America
Thomson Learning
Seneca, 53
Colonia Polanco
11560 Mexico D.F.
Mexico

Spain/Portugal
Paraninfo Thomson Learning
Calle/Magallanes, 25
28015 Madrid, Spain

For Justin Sullivan,
Fear is the only enemy that I still know
--RBT

For Emily and Joshua,
There is no love so deep as mine for you
--DMH

Contents

Preface
    Philosophy As Vision
    Citations and Abbreviations
    Acknowledgments

1. Lives in Transition: Experiencing James   **1**
    William of Albany and the "Prodigal" Son   2
    Henry's "Vastation"   3
    A Battle for the Soul   4
    The First Vocational Turn: Art and Its Foibles   5
    The Second Vocational Turn: Science, Illness   5
    Medicine and Breakdown   7
    The Metaphysical Club, a Budding Career, and Love   9
    Professional Philosophy   11
    Psychic Research, the *Principles*, and Publication   12
    Introducing 'Pragmatism' and the Gifford Lectures   14
    Working Hard, Then Wearing Out   15

2. Taking Philosophy Personally: Psychology, Radical Empiricism, and a Return to Life   **18**
    The Philosophy of James's Psychology   19
    James's Radical Turn   24
    Committing to Experience   25
    A World Purely of Experience   28
    Returning to Life   31

**3. Philosophy in Action: William James and
   Pragmatism**   **34**
    The Origins of Pragmatism   35
    James's Pragmatism   39
    The Career of Pragmatism   51

4. Pluralism and the Moral Life   **56**
    Moral Experience   56
    Determinism, Possibility, and Pluralism   58
    The Moral Life   64
    Meliorism   69

**5. Religious Commitment to a Moral Universe: James
   and "The Will to Believe"**   **76**
    Preliminaries   76
    Against Evidentialism   82
    Faith and Risk   85
    The Case for Religious Belief   86

Selected Works for Further Reading   **92**

Preface

For the philosophy which is so important in each of us is not a technical matter; it is our more or less dumb sense of what life deeply and honestly means.

—"The Present Dilemma in Philosophy" (WWJ, 362)

Philosophy As Vision

William James (1842-1910) is by any reasonable standard the most influential thinker that America has yet produced. In addition to his pioneering role in developing the distinctively American philosophical approach known as Pragmatism, his seminal work, *Principles of Psychology* (1890), established the modern discipline of Experimental Psychology. James also authored the English-language classic in Comparative Religion, *The Varieties of Religious Experience* (1902). Furthermore, his many essays and lectures confront a diverse range of topics of both academic and popular interest, and his presence is to this day strongly felt in every field to which he applied himself.[1]

However, it is this broad scope of James's genius that complicates our task and creates difficulty in doing justice to the mind of William James in fewer than one hundred pages, and yet, that is our charge. Thus, our presentation will involve a considerable degree of selection. Others have presented the whole of James's thought in more comprehensive fashions than we can do here (see, for example, the selected resources at the end of this book). Since the series for which our volume is produced concerns, first and foremost, philosophical themes, we have decided to focus upon the more traditionally philosophical aspects of his work. That is, our primary aims are to situate William James within the Western Philosophical tradition and to encourage and enable further study of

James's thought. Accordingly, we have elected to examine carefully the depth of James's radical empiricism, pragmatism, and moral philosophy. Of course, we shall engage with James's psychology and religious insights, for these endeavors are important to understanding the whole of James's thought. However, we can only do so in the context of this philosophical project and, at times, only incidentally.

We see our study of James emphasizing "philosophy as vision," and while apt, this calls for some explanation. As we read him, James's primary concern is *not* simply to argue for a set of philosophical theses. Though James certainly *does* promote philosophical claims—among them the controversial view of truth for which he is well known—this is not the principal objective of his philosophical thinking. As we intend to emphasize throughout, James insisted that philosophical reflection is never merely an academic exercise but a psychological necessity, a natural process continuous with other life functions. It is the purpose of philosophical activity, as James liked to put it, to make us "feel at home" in the world (WTB, 119), to generate, what he called in another context, the "sentiment of rationality" (WWJ, 317-345).

James's philosophy is in the first instance a *vision*, a way of understanding ourselves. "Philosophy" is another name for what James called life in the "strenuous mood" (WWJ, 627-629), a mood which motivates our life-activities. As such, James saw philosophy as the *attempt* to come to terms with the human condition. Thus it is only secondarily that James's philosophy is expressible as a set of propositions; sophisticated principles and intricate arguments become, then, the *products* of the philosophical enterprise. We aim to convey in this book James's radical vision of philosophy as a *living* and hence *continuing* endeavor to confront directly and honestly the facts of human experience "in all their crude variety" (WWJ, 364).

Our examination of James begins in chapter 1 with a biographical sketch that highlights the very personal, sometimes painful, motivations for James's philosophical thought. Whereas previous commentators (and even, at times, James himself) emphasized radical empiricism as specific metaphysical or epistemological doctrines, we take radical empiricism to be, in part, James's response to his personal travails, an attitude of commitment to lived experience, the insistence upon the reality of relations, transitions, risks, hopes, and joys that we undergo and encounter.

The radically empirical attitude comes to its fullest expression in James's pragmatism, which is the topic of our second chapter. Though it is not uncommon to hear pragmatism criticized for being overly concerned with "getting things done," we here employ the more neutral (we think more fair) characterization of pragmatism as a philosophy of *action*. This philosophical framework of pragmatism, which connects meaning and truth to action and behavior, provides the background for what we take to be the most fascinating aspect of James's thought, namely, his philosophical reflections on the moral life. Thus, our study culminates in the final chapters with an examination of James's meliorism and his defense of religious belief.

Citations and Abbreviations

Since our intended audiences are students and interested general readers, we have elected to key our citations of James's work to the most readily available sources.[2] While several James collections are available in many bookstores, John McDermott's *The Writings of William James: A Comprehensive Edition* is without a doubt the most widely available and useful anthology of James's philosophical work. Thus, wherever possible, we have chosen to cite this edition. However, since some of the essays we cite are not included in McDermott's anthology, we have keyed a few citations to other available editions.

The following abbreviations are used throughout.

Works of James

Full bibliographic information is available at the end of the book under "Selected Works for Further Reading."

Correspondence	*The Correspondence of William James* (vols. 1and4)
PP1	*The Principles of Psychology* (vol. 1)
WJW	*William James: Writings, 1878-1899* (Myers, ed.)
WTB	*The Will to Believe and Other Essays...* (Dover)
WWJ	*The Writings of William James* (McDermott, ed.)

Works of Peirce

V#.Para#	*The Collected Papers of Charles Sanders Peirce.* Vols. 1-6, C. Hartshorne and P. Weiss, eds. (1931, 1932); Vols. 7-8, A. Burks, ed, (1957, 1958). Harvard University Press.

Acknowledgments

The authors have incurred several shared professional debts in the production of this text. In particular, Profs. John J. McDermott, Linda Simon, and Henry Jackman read through the work bringing their impressive knowledge of James to bear. We have also benefited from the comments of our friends and colleagues, James Bednar, Karen Kovach, Dwight Goodyear, Ed Taylor, and Robert Tempio. Furthermore, Prof. William Gavin did us a great service locating a few citations.

Portions of this text were presented by Robert Talisse as part of the Creative Minds Humanities Lecture Series at Amarillo College in Texas, February of 2002. The authors would like to thank everyone at Amarillo College, and especially the Series organizer, Carol Nicklaus, for providing a nearly ideal forum for fine-tuning the ideas articulated in this book.

Thanks are due also to Daniel Kolak, series editor of the Wadsworth Philosophers Series, and everyone at Wadsworth for their guidance.

Finally, the authors have incurred several personal debts as well. Robert Talisse would like to thank Joanne Billett for her continuing support. In addition, Talisse would like to thank Angelo Juffras, who introduced him to the work of William James many years ago. Micah Hester is deeply and happily in the debt of his wife, Kelly Sherman-Hester, who raises their beautiful children, Emily and Joshua (the latter being born during the time this book was written), and constantly lends her love and support to his work. Furthermore, Hester would like to offer his sincere appreciation to John Lachs and Michael Hodges for introducing him to the thought and character of William James.

Endnotes

[1] In 1999 James's *Varieties* placed second on a list of the best English-language, non-fiction books of the 20th century by the editorial board of The Modern Library. His book *Pragmatism* would also have been included were there not a rule excluding multiple listings by the same author (cf. http://www.salon.com/books/log/1999/04/30/modern). Further, James's first book, *Principles of Psychology*, constitutes volume 53 of Encyclopedia Britannica's "Great Books" series.

[2] Unfortunately, most of the volumes published by Harvard University Press as the critical edition of James's writings (1975-1988) are out of print with no plans for reissuing these editions in the near future.

1

Lives in Transition: Experiencing James

[B]uilding up an author's meaning out of separate texts leads nowhere, unless you have fist grasped his centre of vision, by an act of imagination.

—Letter to a student, 1909[1]

The experiences and tensions of William James's life are the source of his philosophical insights. No man has seen better the deep connection between philosophy and lived experience, and James's own life experience strained by powerful conflicts make his life story, and therefore his philosophy, a unique exploration. He was a brilliant man, raised in an exceptional and unique family, whose religious education ran headlong into his scientific pursuits, whose personal crises of depression and anxiety, along with his own curative prescriptions were profoundly influential in his work.

Few American academics, not to mention that subset known as "philosophers," have had the biographical attention heaped upon William James since his death in the summer of 1910. It is no exaggeration to note that dozens of books, chapters, essays, websites, etc. have focused on the details of his remarkable life (this does not include the hundreds of works that speak primarily to his ideas). This is no accident, for James grew up in an exciting time in American history, in a fascinating and impressive

1

family, and with relations and conditions that make James's personal history grand fodder for biography.[2]

William of Albany and the "Prodigal" Son

To understand anyone requires a view of that person in context, and for William James, the philosopher, this context begins to take shape with the story of his grandfather, William James of Albany. The elder William, virtually penniless, immigrated to the United States from Ireland in 1789. However, he turned out to be a shrewd businessman who became one of the wealthiest men in the state of New York.

In part, Grandfather James's work ethic arose from a strong Calvinism, and this religious sensibility also supported his desire to control his environment. William ran a strict household based on an abiding love of a powerful God who demanded effort on His behalf, but it was William's fourth son, Henry James (Sr., later to become father of our own William James), whose spirited youthful vibrancy most directly threatened the disciplined Calvinistic life his father tried to impose.

As he grew up, Henry played the role of the "prodigal son" by following his muse to write and philosophize rather than pursuing the study of business and law favored by his father.

Upon the death of the elder William James in 1832, Henry found himself cut out of his father's three-million-dollar fortune, the two never having reconciled their differences. Undeterred, Henry (along with his half-brother, also named William) brought suit against the estate ultimately winning a share of the bounty—approximately ten thousand dollars per year.[3] This funding afforded Henry the luxury of the contemplative life he desired, and to that end Henry decided to attend Princeton Theological Seminary.

Though theologically inclined and philosophically attuned, Henry was not destined for the life of a minister, nor for that matter, the life of an academic. The Calvinist strictures and self-righteousness of Princeton grew tiresome, and Henry in 1837 took leave of his studies in order to travel. This would be the first of many trips to Europe that Henry would make as he exercised the restless constitution that had long defined him, a constitution he would pass on to his eldest son. By 1838 Henry was back in the States but left Princeton, turning instead to what he considered to be purely philosophical endeavors.

Before leaving seminary, however, Henry was introduced to Mary Walsh, and romance ensued. But while Henry sported his own good looks and an out-going, energetic personality, Mary was by all accounts no great beauty and neither animated nor jovial. Even so (or maybe, in response), Henry's passion for Mary ran deep, and in 1840 they were married. This union made for a fortuitous coupling, for while Henry tended toward the excessive, Mary's practical, shrewd character kept such excesses in check.

Without need to work and with Henry's unsettled spirit, the new couple moved between Albany and New York City for several years, staying with family, in a rented flat of their own, as well as in the luxurious Astor House Hotel. It was there on January 11, 1842 that their first son, William James, was born, and within six years, the family would be filled with four more children—Henry (1843-1916), Garth Wilkinson (1845-1883), Robertson (1846-1910), and Alice (1848-1892).

Henry's "Vastation"

William's pre-adolescent years are marked more by the concerns and events of his father's life than of his own. Henry James, Sr. was a man in search—in search of insight into human life and religious understanding, in search of recognition by other "intellectuals" (in particular, such New England intellectuals as Emerson, Alcott, and Thoreau), and in search of home. These searches led his restless spirit to wander, both mentally and physically, and these wanderings implicated others. Henry often displaced his family moving between the United States and Europe, typically to alleviate his own frustrations with his philosophical work or family dynamics.

Henry was prone to mood swings and a pivotal moment came one night in May of 1844. After dinner Henry sat alone

> when suddenly—in a lightning flash, as it were—"fear came upon me, and trembling, which made all my bones shake." To all appearances it was a perfectly insane and abject terror, without ostensible cause, and only to be accounted for, to my perplexed imagination, by some damnèd shape squatting invisible to me with the precincts of the room, and raying out from his fetid personality influences fatal to life. (WWJ, 3)

This event had a powerful effect on Henry, launching him into his deepest depression.

Seeking specialists to help him, Henry found his "cure" through an introduction to the philosophy of Swedish mystic, Emanuel Swedenborg.

In particular, Swedenborg posited the concept of "vastation"—a catharsis that leads to positive ends—and Henry came to see his own moment of dreadful anxiety as his personal vastation. Further, in Swedenborgianism Henry found a philosophy that unburdened any remaining Calvinist guilt, for Swedenborg believed that since selfhood came from the universal God, it could not be individually unique. Each of us, in essence, is equal and divine. Swedenborgianism gave Henry a renewed spirit and a new concern for social justice, for Henry saw that, at his/her core, no individual was better than another, and all this conspired to provide a new sense of purpose.

A Battle for the Soul

One aspect of Henry's new purpose was the "proper" enlightenment of his own children. This translated into an almost schizophrenic philosophy of education, wherein innocence was to be protected and a free mind was to be fostered at all cost. This resulted in Henry's constant discontentment with William's studies as William passed between tutor and private school and back, several times. However, during his second European trip in the mid-1850s, the out-going, almost gregarious, William found some stability and ability in his education becoming fluent in French, exercising his talents in art, and finding an abiding interest in science as well. But so long as he remained under his father's rule, his ability to strive in any one direction would be difficult, for Henry's insistence on a protracted innocence *demanded* a continually open mind to the infinite possibilities of life.

Eventually, Henry settled the family in Newport, and once again, set up a tutorial system of education for William. As part of this education, and to continue his efforts in the arts, William took classes from resident artist, William Morris Hunt. As an artist, William was finding his place. Hunt's personality and instruction were well received by the young man, but father Henry was less enthusiastic about his eldest son's ever-clearing focus. Henry's own desire for William was to become a scientist in the mode of Thoreau, to gather and extend knowledge in and through nature. Art would never do for such a noble and vital purpose.

Henry's ideas concerning art, science, and philosophy changed confusingly over his lifetime, but it seems that he made no clean divide between science and art while clearly both the professional artist and the professional scientist were suspect. While art and science implicated each other through technology—i.e., control over nature—and while this control was seen by Henry as a God-given ability that should be exercised, the vocational artist's soul was too caught up with prestige while the working scientist was too concerned with the mundane for either ever to reach the spiritual heights envisaged by Henry.

The First Vocational Turn: Art and Its Foibles

Initially, Henry lost this battle and after a year-long hiatus in Switzerland (1859-1860), William eagerly followed his passion for art under Hunt's tutelage. However, while William was away in Europe, Hunt's work as a portrait artist had taken off. This gave William insight into the practical concerns of the artist that reached far beyond the choice of color and paint. William began to realize that artistry, like his own father's oratory, concerned not just himself but his audience. No work, not even the lofty heights of the artist, was detachable from everyday concerns—economics, social graces, personality.

Meanwhile, Henry James did not let up on William, still hoping that he would turn away from his passion and towards the intellectual life of science—and not in the laboratory, but in the field. Knowledge as the pursuit of the soul, not the pursuit of particular goals, was Henry's ideal. What mattered is that activity pushes out from the passions of the soul in order to gain intellectual insight into spiritual matters. William was never oblivious to his father's spiritual concerns.

Within a year, William's interest in art waned. Stimulated primarily by his own self-doubt over his abilities, William worried about his success as an artist and his ability to pay for such a lifestyle.[4] Never having dropped his joy in science and experimentation, thoughts of academic studies in the sciences began to take hold evermore strongly. Thus, in 1861 when his father made William a deal that he could enroll at the Lawrence Scientific School in Cambridge, Massachusetts rather than enlist for service in the Civil War, William jumped at the opportunity.[5]

This decisive moment in many ways closed the chapter on the external battle between father and son for William's soul, but the internal battle within William himself was still in its infancy, and its climax remained almost a decade away.

The Second Vocational Turn: Science, Illness

In the Fall of 1861, William James entered the Lawrence Scientific School to study first chemistry, then anatomy and biology. There William's study under anatomist Jeffries Wyman was most influential.

On James

Wyman accepted evolutionary theory and taught the basic theory to the young William (William entered Lawrence only two years after the publication of Darwin's *On The Origin of Species*). Evolutionary theory from then on became a central influence in William's work in physiology, psychology, and philosophy.

William became fully immersed in the kind of formal study he craved; however, even this did not thwart a nagging despair that loomed constantly over the young man. It was clear even to his teachers that, as his chemistry professor Charles Eliot put it, "his work was much interfered by ill-health, or rather by something which I imagined to be a delicacy of nervous constitution."

Coupled with this decline of mental stability were financial concerns of his parents that motivated a new direction. In 1864, upon the urging of Wyman, William entered Harvard Medical School. Rather than contiguous, uninterrupted study in medicine, however, in 1865 William followed the charismatic biologist Louis Agassiz to Brazil for an extended expedition. Though he enjoyed the country and its people, William was thoroughly uninterested in the activities of a biologist, and he was clearly in stark disagreement with Agassiz's placement of biology under the care of divine revelation. In a letter home, he even mentions that such work had made him certain that philosophy should be his true pursuit (Correspondence 1:8). Furthermore, during the trip William came down with a form of smallpox that hospitalized him and left him temporarily blinded. Along with mental troubles, physical illness, including problems with vision, would recur throughout the remainder of his life.

The recurrence of illness is evidenced within a year of his return from Brazil in 1866, and regularly for six years beyond, William spent five of them battling illness, alternating between affliction and convalescence, and back. The symptoms were depression, irritability, back pain, and gastric disruption, and again, like his father, such critical times called for changes in scenery. Seeking a respite for his depression, a balm for his aching back, and an opportunity to learn the German language better, William set out in the spring of 1867 for Dresden, but there he found no relief from his pain and anguish.

It was during this time, however, that he began to turn critical attention to his father's work, and in so doing, repudiated his father's belief that complete subjugation of the self to God was the only path to true moral and spiritual peace. If we are to achieve anything we might call "moral," he argued, we must do so through our own efforts. *"Everything* we know and are is through men," he stated in a letter of 1868. "We have no revelation but through man. Every sentiment that warms your gizzard every brave act that ever made your pulse bound and your nostril open to a confident breath was a man's act. However mean a man may be, man is *the best we know*" (Correspondence, 4:249).

This potency of human power would persist not only in William's writings, but in his life as well. However, no amount of will power was yet able to turn the tide of depression, and he wrote his father from Berlin that "the pistol the dagger and the bowl began to usurp an unduly large part of my attention" (Correspondence, 4:194). This would not be the last consideration of suicide William would utter, but clinging to his faith in the power of human effort kept him from succumbing to such thoughts.

During his years in Europe, William took the time, even in the midst of depression, to study. Of particular interest to his later work was a brief time spent in Heidelberg studying physiology under Hermann von Helmholtz and psychology with Wilhelm Wundt. While these contacts were disappointingly underdeveloped for William, the influence of Helmholtz and Wundt was decisive in his approach to physiology, an approach that evolved quickly into experimental psychology, resulting in the first academic recognition of the latter field at Harvard during the 1870s and, later, William's own seminal two-volume work, *Principles of Psychology*. Such results, however, were still years off, and though the germination process had begun, William had yet to light upon its importance to his career direction. Instead, he decided that the "vagabond life" was not for him, and in the fall of 1868, he moved back to the United States.

Medicine and Breakdown

Standing for examination a few months after his return, William was granted the degree of doctor of medicine in June of 1869, but even such an accomplishment could not pull him out of his depression. From the time of his Brazilian trip in 1865, William's back had given him troubles. Further, his mood had been in decline since at least the earlier part of the decade, and not his travels in Europe, his accomplishments in academics, nor his time with friends and family could bring him back. When his pain had reached its epitome, the depths of his mood were not far behind. In the winter of 1870 James wrote in his journal,

> Today I about touched bottom, and perceived plainly that I
> must face the choice with open eyes: shall I frankly throw the

moral business [read: "my father's vocational pursuits"] over-
board, as one unsuited to my innate aptitudes, or shall I follow
it, and it alone, making everything unsuited to it? (WWJ, 7)

"Touching bottom" was profoundly disturbing. Many years later, in
The Varieties of Religious Experience he wrote autobiographically,[6]

> Whilst in this state of philosophical pessimism and general
> depression of spirits about my prospects, I went one evening
> into a dressing-room in the twilight to procure some article
> that was there; when suddenly there fell upon me without any
> warning, just as if it came out of the darkness, a horrible fear
> of my own existence. Simultaneously there arose in my mind
> the image of an epileptic patient whom I had seen in the asy-
> lum.... He sat there like a sort of Egyptian cat or Peruvian
> mummy, moving nothing but his black eyes and looking abso-
> lutely non-human. This image and my fear entered into a spe-
> cies of combination with each other. *That shape am I*, I felt,
> potentially.... After this the universe was changed for me al-
> together. I awoke morning after morning with a horrible
> dread at the pit of my stomach, and with a sense of the insecu-
> rity of life that I never knew before....
>   In general I dreaded to be left alone. I remember wonder-
> ing how other people could live, how I myself had ever lived,
> so unconscious of that pit of insecurity beneath the surface of
> life. (WWJ, 6)

This account, uncannily similar to that of his father's own "vastation," displays the signs of deep pathology. His mood became what he
would later call, "an essentially religious disease" the cure for which
seemingly was either to accept nature *qua* "hard facts," as the purely scientific mind does, or to admit of the possibility of religious salvation.
And though the decline into depression was at least a decade in reaching
bottom, the ascent to more affable heights came rather quickly. Surely
among other cures, William's deliverance came from philosophic study
and personal belief in human power. He wrote in late April of 1870:

> I think that yesterday was a crisis in my life. I finished the
> first part of Renouvier's second "Essais" and see no reason
> why his definition of Free Will—"the sustaining of a thought
> because I choose to when I might have other thoughts"—need

8

be the definition of an illusion. At any rate, I will assume for the present—until next year—that it is no illusion. My first act of free will shall be to believe in free will.... Not in maxims, not in *Anschauungen* [perceptions, intuitions], but in accumulated acts of thought lies salvation.... Hitherto, when I have felt like taking a free initiative,...suicide seemed the most manly form to put my daring into; now, I will go a step further with my will, not only to act with it, but to believe as well; believe in my individual reality and creative power.... Life shall be built in doing and suffering and creating. (WWJ, 7-8)

William thus took a novel tact, namely, to believe in the possibility that his own actions have the power to bring about salvation—otherwise unrealizable without effort. If the world is indeed the precarious and chaotic place that lights upon our senses, then no amount of certitude will resolve our concerns and wipe away our fears. "[O]ften enough our faith beforehand in an uncertified result is *the only thing that makes the result come true*" (WTB, 59).

The Metaphysical Club, a Budding Career, and Love

Even during his years of depression, William could be easily animated by philosophical discussion. In particular, William found the banter and argument of his good friend Oliver Wendell Holmes, Jr. (not yet Supreme Court Justice) stimulating and penetrating. He also gained deep insight from his former student-colleague, chemist, mathematician, and philosopher Charles Peirce. The presence of John Fiske, a philosophical historian, and Chauncey Wright, a scientist and philosopher, could also make for an evening of insightful debate. These untrained philosophical men and others formed what they called the "Metaphysical Club," and they spent much of the 1870s debating the virtues of positivism, rationalism, and what came to be called pragmatism.

To give himself some monetary and vocational stability, in 1871 William accepted an appointment as instructor in anatomy and physiology, but from the first was not convinced of its staying power. Almost immediately, he began to lament his decision to leave art, while his philosophical pursuits continued as well. He wrote in his journal about the hope of one day finding an appointment in philosophy, believing physiol-

9

ogy and anatomy too confining a discipline. By 1873, his depression was back and, once again, he was off to Europe to find renewed health and to visit his increasingly successful and *younger* brother, Henry (Jr—well-known novelist).

William's once close relationship with his brother had become strained and would continue to show signs of jealousy and misunderstanding for the rest of their years. Henry found a home as an expatriate in Europe and discovered his muse in short stories and novels. William, though deeply influenced by his many travels abroad, and never quite able to shake wanderlust, was never happy with extended time away from the United States and never came to grips with his own brother's love of Europe. Also, the many letters between William and Henry demonstrate what can only be called William's patronizing attitude towards Henry's writings, always critical, looking for Henry to provide more direct prose and insight—criticism that Henry always suffered kindly. The irony, however, is many-fold, for while William was known throughout Europe in his day as the quintessential American philosophical voice, he has been called by some American theorists as the most European of American philosophers. Also, his writings are well known for their liberal use of literary prose rather than logical analysis, a practice that has led to criticism concerning lack of precision and clarity in the face of difficult conceptual matters.

Aside from bringing into strong relief his personal connection to America and only partially reinvigorating his relationship with Henry, the trip proved otherwise unsuccessful at providing William with the answers and resolutions to his depression and despair that he sought. After a year's absence, William returned to teaching in hopes of grounding his wandering spirit. It worked. From 1874 until his retirement, William was never unemployed again. Taking on more responsibility and effort at Harvard proved a cure for his current depression, and his efforts resulted in initiative. By 1875, William was reconstructing his coursework by evolving his lectures in physiology into the first academic discussions in the United States concerning experimental psychology and its philosophical implications.

But those academic, scholarly paths paled in comparison to his fortunate introduction to Alice Howe Gibbens in the spring of 1876. Alice was an intelligent, insightful, 26 year old woman grounded by her belief in God, with a pleasant sense of humor and critical wit that kept William on his toes. After two years of courtship, they were married, and the marriage was, to its end, a partnership. Even in work, William and Alice collaborated—William would dictate while Alice transcribed *and* responded. The marriage also would produce five offspring, four of whom would survive to adulthood—Henry (1879-1947), William (1882-1961), Herman (1884-85), Margaret Mary (1887-1950), and Alexander (1890-1946).

Professional Philosophy

Aside from his marriage, the year 1878 marked a turning point in William's life as his academic work made headway. In January of 1878, the *Journal of Speculative Philosophy* published William's first signed publication, "Remarks on Spencer's Definition of Mind as Correspondence." Therein, William takes on the philosophy and psychology of Hebert Spencer (1820-1903), work he had been closely acquainted with for nearly a decade. While supporting the Darwinian foundation of Spencer's thought, William criticizes, among other things, what he sees as Spencer's reductionist conclusions that human beings are at bottom survivalists, and their nature is geared only to protection and procreation. William saw this narrowing of human experience as mistaken. Informed by his reading of French philosopher, Charles Renouvier (1818-1903) and professing a theme that resurfaced throughout his psychological and philosophical writings, William stresses that human activity, and the efforts put forth, are a wildcard that cannot, a priori, be "knowable." Furthermore, experience shows us that many interests, not just survival, conspire in the individual to give life it richness and flavor—an inextractible richness.

> If ministry to survival be the sole criterion of mental excellence, then luxury and amusement, Shakespeare, Beethoven, Plato, and Marcus Aurelius, stellar spectroscopy, diatom markings, and nebular hypotheses are by-products on too wasteful a scale. The slag-heap is too big—it abstracts more energy than it contributes to the ends of the machine. (WJW, 901)

Arguing that such "excesses" of the Spencerian scale cannot merely be superfluous, "truth" can never be mere "correspondence," for our interests extend beyond mere survival in the face of what is "given." Our "mental interests, hypotheses, postulates, so far as they are bases for human action—action which to a great extent transforms the world—help make the truth which they declare" (WJW, 908).

11

In the same year, John Fiske (from the Metaphysical Club) put William in contact with the publisher Henry Holt who was looking to produce a textbook in psychology. William was eager to set forth his thoughts on the topic, hoping to create a volume that would provide sufficient funding for his family. And while the project became quite protracted, its definitive and seminal results are unmistakable, namely, the 1890 publication of the two-volume, *Principles of Psychology*.

Meanwhile, in 1879 William published more essays, most importantly, "The Sentiment of Rationality" wherein he argues for the place of the affective dimensions in inquiry where the "feeling" of contentment is our sign of resolution to what his friend Charles Peirce called the "irritation of doubt" (5.358-387). Such work, along with his own resolve to shift disciplines achieved William's coveted position of assistant professor of philosophy at Harvard in 1880 where he continued to serve for more than 25 years, a time rightly chronicled as a golden age in the department. During those years, James would help Josiah Royce gain a post, teach, among others, George Santayana, Gertrude Stein, Ralph Barton Perry, W. E. B. Du Bois, and William Ernest Hocking, and become the foremost advocate of pragmatism, influencing the likes of John Dewey and George Herbert Mead.

Psychic Research, the *Principles*, and Publication

In the mid-1880s William's interest turned to, among other things, psychical research, or "spiritualism." The fascination with mediums and psychics was of great curiosity to many in the late nineteenth century with eminent academics and laypersons coming together to learn about and investigate the claims of spiritual phenomena. In one sense this work would seem at odds with a philosopher whose own work in psychology was sometimes thought to be too physiological.[7] But, as would be a point he made often, physiology (as a solely materialist position) did not exhaust explanations of experience. Between his own confused spiritual inheritance from his father and his never-ending pursuit of the truths which lie in all corners of experience, William kept open the possibility of psychic ability and phenomena until his death, helping to establish the American Society for Psychical Research and setting up a laboratory for psychic experimentation at Harvard. Upon the premature death of his third son, Herman, in 1885, William and his wife Alice even became regular clients of a trance medium named Leonora Piper.

While he longed for recognition and continued to look for positions elsewhere, the remainder of the decade saw William solidifying his place at Harvard, and after yet another trip to Europe, he came home to focus on the completion of *Principles of Psychology*, promised over a decade earlier. In 1890 the literary, psychological, and philosophical masterpiece William had hoped to create came to fruition. Though its size is imposing, its prose, insight, and argument are intoxicating. In the English language, no work before it had taken on the subject of psychology to the degree and with the concern for empirical evidence that William presented. It offers a radical view of the self, mind, thought, and experience in a comprehensive manner. William's *Principles* undermines the idea of a self which is ontologically prior to experience, emphasizing instead what he called the "stream of thought." This "stream" when uninterrupted admits of no division into subjective and objective elements, but when interrupted is redirected by reflective processes that function to "fit" experiences together in order to continue the flow. He explains how habits (physiological, biological, and emotional) play an important instrumental role as the primary controlling mechanism and expression of the self. In other words, William insisted that any analysis of psychology be a "functional" one whereby the living, concrete individual as an active being within an influencing environment is taken seriously. The ideas were revolutionary and widely influential.

Though he readily wanted to take on new projects, particularly more squarely in philosophy, the desire to make the *Principles* more accessible to the classroom had William back at his desk paring down, revising, rewriting, and adding to his two-volume set. The product was his one-volume 1892 *Psychology (Briefer Course)*, which became an English-language textbook standard for decades to come. The fame that this and the earlier work gave him created the opportunity for regular speaking engagements, and much of his published output for the rest of his life would have its genesis (if not its culmination) in the lecture hall. In fact, he would not again publish a book in his lifetime that did not originate from such sources, or as collections of journal articles.[8]

Unfortunate news came in the Spring of 1892 when William's sister Alice died from breast cancer. His relationship to Alice was long strained as she went through years of tortured mental and physical problems that, though he should have had great sympathy for, he never truly understood. Her (published) diaries, for which she is justly praised in literary circles, testify to a woman of intelligence, depth, and courage in the face of great adversity. They also give insight to her family, and William's distance over the years was, it is clear, not simply geographical.

The years that followed found William, while still relying on his studies in psychology, moving into more philosophical pursuits. Such thoughts culminated in the 1897 collection of his writings entitled *The Will to Believe and Other Essays in Popular Philosophy*. Full of important pieces previously published such as "The Sentiment of Rationality" (1879-1882), "The Dilemma of Determinism" (1884), "The Moral Philosopher and the Moral Life" (1891), "Is Life Worth Living?" (1895), as well as the famous title piece (and the focus of our final chapter), "The Will to Believe" (1896), the collection was dedicated to William's old friend, Charles Peirce, "To whose philosophic comradeship in old times and to whose writings in more recent years I owe more incitement and help than I can express or repay." William had long been a champion of Peirce, especially in Peirce's struggle to find a permanent faculty appointment. While a brilliant scientist and philosopher, Peirce's hindrance to this goal was his own personality that was simply intolerable to most people. However, on more than one occasion (and without success), William put Peirce's name forth to hire at Harvard, and in 1893 even suggested Peirce to head the newly forming department of philosophy at the University of Chicago (an appointment that would eventually go to John Dewey).

Introducing 'Pragmatism' and the Gifford Lectures

The decade ended with William working too hard for his physical and emotional constitution, lecturing often. His own concern for his health and finances led him initially to turn down an invitation to give the prestigious Gifford Lectures in Natural Religion at the University of Edinburgh, suggesting instead his colleague, friend, and philosophical nemesis, Josiah Royce.[9] However, the university persisted and made arrangements for two series of lectures in 1899-1901.

The years 1898-1899 proved pivotal, beginning with the development of a heart ailment that would prove chronic and, ultimately, fatal. However, even with this William traveled to California where he gave a series of lectures at the Universities of California at Berkeley and Los Angeles. Notably, it was during this series that William gave a lecture, published immediately thereafter as "Philosophical Conceptions and Practical Results," in which he first used the term 'pragmatism' to denote a theory of truth wherein the "meaning" of a concept is marked by "some particular consequence, in our future practical experience, whether active or passive; the point lying rather in the fact that the experience must be particular, than in the fact that it must be active" (WWJ, 349). This consequentialist take on truth and meaning, William believed, was simply a restatement of Charles Peirce's own principle of practicalism concerning the meaning of our beliefs. This important concept would later be fleshed out in William's famous 1907 lectures entitled *Pragmatism*, but the relevant "principle" is instrumental throughout much of his writings before and after 1898.

By 1899, he was off again to Europe working on his Gifford lectures, due to be given starting in January 1900. The task was daunting, and because of his health, the lectures had to be postponed until 1901, but the result was another impressive and definitive work. A psychological sociology of religious insights and practices, *The Varieties of Religious Experience* has proved virtually as influential as his landmark *Principles*. Beginning with a psychological development of religious experience—dividing human religious appreciation between the "healthy-minded" and "sick souls"—and after a survey of religious phenomenologies from "conversion" to "mysticism," William concludes that

> the only thing that [religious experience] testifies to is that we can experience union with *something* larger than ourselves and in that union find our greatest peace.... It need not be infinite, it need not be solitary. It might conceivably even be only a larger and more godlike self. (WWJ, 785-786).

Exorcising the spiritual demons that long possessed him, William's conclusions carefully leave room for the gods of both his grandfather *and* father while opening "spiritual" space for the "godlike" aspects of human association, personal transcendence, and his own "willful" and "pragmatic" view of religious belief.

Working Hard, Then Wearing Out

The ensuing years were marked by more travel, tenuous health, and continuing lecturing. He spent the spring of 1905 traveling Europe, meeting with Henri Bergson (1859-1941) in France and a group of Italian philosophers, headed by pragmatist Giovanni Papini (1881-1956). The following winter William was a visiting professor at Stanford University, where in February 1906 he delivered his well-received lecture, "The

15

Moral Equivalent of War," wherein he argued that the aggressive, warlike element of our character is ingrained in us, expressing itself in what he called the "martial virtues"—for example, "intrepidity, contempt of softness, surrender of private interest, obedience to command" (WWJ, 668). Unable to give up such virtues but desirous of eschewing the blood bath that is war, William suggested that we retrain our habits in "moral equivalents," like conquering nature or forging stronger bonds of community.

By 1907 William prepared to shift gears once again. After several years of debate with Harvard administration, William finally took retirement at the end of January. With his teaching duties behind him, he was able to turn his attention to the publication of his book, *Pragmatism*, the result of his Lowell Lectures at Boston and Columbia Universities (we address the basic arguments of the lectures in the next chapter). This completed the disciplinary triumvirate in his bibliography—first psychology, then religion, finally philosophy.

In his final years, William, though constantly in ill health, continued lecturing while defending his work from critics, most of whom espoused an idealism that was at odds with his more empirically grounded work. Affording him another trip abroad, he gave and published (in 1909) the Hibbert Lectures at Manchester College, Oxford under the title, *A Pluralistic Universe*. William also set out to write a comprehensive opus that could stand as his final statement tying up the various concepts he had written about throughout his career—pluralism, radical empiricism, pragmatism, theism, and so forth. The project would never see completion (though an incomplete version was published posthumously in 1911 as *Some Problems in Philosophy*).

One final trip to England occurred in the spring and summer of 1910 in response to pleas from brother Henry who was in ill health. However, William's own health continued its decline, and his heart could no longer sustain him. Within weeks of his arrival back in the States at his country home in Chocorua, New Hampshire, he succumbed to his lasting ailment on August 26, 1910. His wife insightfully recorded the cause in her diary: "Acute enlargement of the heart. He had worn himself out."

Endnotes

[1] Though Henry James, III's collection of letters (*The Letters of William James*, 2 vols. New York: Atlantic Monthly Press, 1926, 355) dates this letter as "May. 26, 1900," the letter is from May 26, 1909

(correction to Simon 1998, 394n11—full citation available at the end of the book in "Selections for Further Reading").

[2] The biographical portions of this section are informed primarily by 4 sources: Simon 1998; Allen 1967; Feinstein 1984; Perry 1935. (Full citations available at the end of the book in "Selections for Further Reading")

[3] H. Feinstein (1984, 58-75) notes that though some money was garnered within a couple of years, the final settlement was not complete until 1846.

[4] The artistic legacy was carried on by two of William's children—both William, Jr. (Billy) and Aleck became quite respectable painters.

[5] The 2 younger brothers, Garth Wilkinson (Wilky) and Robertson (Bob) did enlist, Wilky serving under Col. Robert Gould Shaw with the Massachusetts 54th, the first black regiment.

[6] William's son, Henry, has explained that his father told him that this account, which according to the text is supposedly about a "Frenchman," is in fact about William himself from around 1869-1870.

[7] One example is what is known as the James-Lange theory of emotions, as stated in his famous 1884 article "What Is an Emotion" (and amplified in the chapter (XXV) "The Emotions" in the *Principles*, v2). Therein, James places priority on action over mental states in determining emotion. In particular, he claims that it would be more true to say that, for example, our response of running from a bear is prior to our emotive response of fear, or to put it more succinctly, running simply is the fear prior to our development and subsequent awareness of such a mental process. This physiological explanation gives controllability to emotions, which James would later link to his all-important concept of "habit" which undergirds his philosophy of human potency of action.

[8] Among his later publications are, *The Will to Believe and Other Essays* (1897), *Talks to Teachers on Psychology* (1899), the Gifford Lectures in Natural Philosophy known as *The Varieties of Religious Experience* (1902), the *Pragmatism* Lowell Lectures (1907), *The Meaning of Truth* (1909)—what James called a reply to his critics concerning his Lowell Lectures—*A Pluralistic Universe* (1909), and the posthumously published *Essays in Radical Empiricism* (1912).

[9] Royce gave the lectures in 1899, published under the title, *The World and the Individual*.

2

Taking Philosophy Personally: Psychology, Radical Empiricism, and a Return to Life

If philosophy be really on the eve of any considerable rearrangement, the time should be propitious for any one who has suggestions of his own to bring forth. For many years past my mind has been growing into a certain type of Weltanschauung.... I propose, therefore, ...to throw my description into the bubbling vat of publicity where, jostled by rivals and torn by critics, it will eventually either disappear from notice, or else, if better luck befall it, quietly subside to the profundities, and serve as a possible ferment of new growth or a nucleus of new crystallization.

—"A World of Pure Experience" (WWJ, 195)

As the biographical sketch of the previous chapter begins to demonstrate, James's philosophical insights, his emphasis on human potency in action and the need to take experience seriously arise directly from elements in his own life story. The grandchild of a devoted Calvinist and shrewd businessman, the child of a rebellious "prodigal" son who followed the theoretical muse of a religiously grounded philosophy that ran directly counter to a Calvinist upbringing, William James was an intelligent child unable to light upon his own calling until relatively late in his life. An artist of some talent, a scientist of worthy credentials, James could not easily dive into nor let go of any one set of practices, for fear of differentiating too soon and differentiating too much. For James, more so than many, the tensions between art and science were intimately experienced (and ultimately, convincingly dissolved). Add to this mix a profound concern for the role of religion and spiritual matters, and it is easy enough to see how the "big blooming buzzing confusion" (WWJ, 233) of experience led to a mental breakdown while the infinite possibilities available in experience along with resolve in human potency led him back out of that great despair.

Characteristic of all James's work is the intimate relationship between what he wrote and what he lived. As his friend and colleague, Josiah Royce, wrote, "[James] rediscovered whatever he…received from without; because he never could teach what he had not himself experienced."[1] James turned this personal connection to experience into a philosophically interesting position he called "radical empiricism." Experience, according to James, is a rich "mosaic" with the mortar as directly experienced as the tiles (WWJ, 195). Any pursuit implicates all experience. So it is not surprising that within the fertile mind of William James, his own wide array of interests and experiences, though initially leading to a psychological position, ranged over several disciplines.

However, the psychological basis of radical empiricism may, in fact, be its most important *philosophical* feature. Thus, before we dive headlong into a discussion of radical empiricism, we shall take a short but necessary detour into a few aspects of James's psychology.

The Philosophy of James's Psychology

During James's formative educational years well into his studies for the medical degree, the field of psychology was considered a subdiscipline of philosophy. Thus, most of what was written under the title of "psychology" was, in fact, a form of speculative philosophy concerning what constituted the mind and its functions, typically addressing in turn sensations, perception, and consciousness. However, all that changed during the mid-nineteenth century when the desire to apply scientific methods to psychological questions grew in direct response to the rise of experimental success within many of the sciences. Recall that during James's studies in Germany during the 1860s, he became acquainted with the physiologist Wilhelm Wundt whose groundbreaking volume a decade later, *Grundzüge der physiologischen Psychologie* [*Principles of Physiological Psychology*] (1874), set the international stage for the study of experimental psychology. Meanwhile, James himself began to develop his own thoughts and research in the field, and it is in no small part due to James's studies and writings that psychology broke away from philosophy within the academy. Ironically, however, James himself never strayed far from deeply philosophical concerns when discussing psychology.

James began teaching courses in psychology during the 1870s, adding progressively more research projects to the educational experience, finally culminating in the establishment of the first experimental research lab in psychology in the U.S. Through his work in experimental, physiological psychology and his frustration with "structuralist" (building up the contents of the mind from atomic sensations) and purely "introspective" (relying solely on subjective accounts of private mental states to account for the mind and its functions) approaches in vogue at the time, James put his scientific and medical training in physiology and empirical evidence to work. This led him to an account of psychology that, while indebted to its predecessors, transcended all that had come before and helped launch the influential efforts in late nineteenth and early twentieth century functional and behavioristic psychologies.

In 1890, after 12 years of research, procrastination, frustration, and, of course, writing, William James succeeding in producing what is quite simply the single most important work in the history of American psychology—*The Principles of Psychology*. Initially intended to be a small classroom textbook for Henry Holt publishing, the project expanded to two volumes totaling well over 1000 pages. There simply is no way to do justice to this important work within the few pages allotted for this text. As such, a full account will necessarily give way to a focus on a few aspects of Jamesian psychology (both as reported in the *Principles* and as expanded and evolved in his later writings) that help render and make more accessible philosophical aspects of his work that our text is most directly trying to illuminate for the reader.

In his Preface to the *Principles*, James carefully distinguishes what he calls "metaphysics" (discussion of the existence and nature of thoughts and things known) from psychology (the conditions of the mind and brain that correspond to thoughts and feelings) (PP1, v-vi), and adds that while a metaphysical dualism (such as Rene Descartes [1596-1650] had suggested) is untenable, the psychologist could not but work within such a dualism. In fact, this dualistic divide between philosophy and psychology would continue to press James throughout the *Principles* and later. In response, as early as 1894, James, in his essay "The Knowing of Things Together," would begin to dismantle any vestiges of the psychological dualism in favor of his philosophical pluralism and meliorism.

However, the rejection took some time and strategy, so before we get there, let us explore a few points in the *Principles* for just a moment. As mentioned, the James of the *Principles*, in fact, makes dualism a central feature of psychology, stating, "*The psychologist's attitude towards cognition...is a thoroughgoing dualism.* It supposes two elements, mind knowing and thing known, and treats them as irreducible" (PP1, 218). Here we find James positing boldly the traditional Cartesian dualism between thinker and thing, subject and object. Of course, it is important to note the qualifier that James has slipped in—that is, this dualism is the "psychologist's attitude"—for he claims later, "The dualism of Object and Subject and their pre-established harmony are what the psychologist as such must assume, whatever ulterior monisitc philosophy he may...have in reserve" (PP1, 220). So for James, a non-dualistic metaphysic was not necessarily incompatible with the psychologist's dualistic attitude; but the James of the *Principles* could not allow the psychologist to work outside such a dualism.

This component of his psychology frustrated his philosophical sensibilities, and his own pragmatic attitude honed from years of discussion with the likes of Charles Peirce forced him to reconsider this psychological dualism in light of the continuity between thought and act he himself had seen at the moment of his own greatest despair. He states in the concluding paragraph of "The Knowing of Things Together," "I have become convinced since publishing [the *Principles*] that no conventional restrictions can keep metaphysical and so-called epistemological inquires out of psychology books" (WWJ, 168).

Of course, the seeds of his later psychology are already planted firmly in the *Principles*, not only in its content and argument but also in the very structural organization of the work. Unlike the few psychology textbooks before his, James's *Principles* does not begin with sensations and perceptions, but with physiological discussions of the brain, physiology being nothing more and nothing less than the scientific discipline of anatomical and biological functions. His, then, is a "functional" approach to psychology (though it is John Dewey who is often credited with giving birth to this approach). We see this "functional" character all the more by chapter four when James introduces the all-important concept of habit that remains in the background of the entire work, and for that matter, James's entire corpus. Habit, for James, is a function of life wherein physical bodies respond to given conditions, adjusting as required by those conditions. There is a "plasticity" (PP1, 104-105; WWJ, 10-11) to living things that makes possible habitual life. In the brain, sensations develop neural pathways, either by creating new pathways or by reinvigorating previous ones. Habits are the pathways of least resistance formed by previous sensations and stimulated by given conditions (PP1, 106-109; WWJ, 11-12). Habit, then, allows James to discuss thought physiologically, and adds the important elements of training and character to his psychology (PP1, 120-127; WWJ, 15-21). He contends, "Habit…the enormous fly-wheel of society, its most precious conservative agent," keeping us "within the bounds of ordinance" (PP1, 121; WWJ, 16). Habits make efforts more efficient (PP1, 119-121; WWJ 15-16) while also less conscious (PP1, 114; WWJ, 15). James quotes the Duke of Wellington, "Habit a second nature! Habit is ten times nature" (PP1, 120; WWJ 14). But the power of habit is a double-edged sword, the key being " to *make our nervous system our ally instead of our enemy*" (PP1, 122; WWJ, 17). Education of habits, then, is of utmost importance, and the effect on our character is unquestionably vital. Thus, he says, "*Seize the very first possible opportunity to act on every resolution you make and on every emotional prompting you may experience in the direction of the habits you aspire to gain*" (PP1, 124; WWJ, 18).

By the time he addresses the concept of "consciousness," James's functional apparatus has laid the groundwork for the bold claim that "consciousness is at all times primarily *a selecting agency*" (PP1, 139). This claim will be made even more radical and functional in James's later work "Does 'Consciousness' Exist?," but even here, it is no small point to note James's choice of "agency" over "agent" ('agency', as the *Oxford Universal Dictionary* tells us, is defined as "action personified"). The *active* character of consciousness as the *defining* character of consciousness makes this an already radical claim, for both traditional rationalism and empiricism simply accepted that the mind was an entity that perceived, thought, reasoned, but that did so as a passive receptor. James's use of "agency" begins the turn that strips the passively substantive characteristic of consciousness away, focusing, instead, on the performative quality of consciousness.

Maybe the most famous chapter in the *Principles* is "The Stream of Thought" (later renamed by James "The Stream of Consciousness" for his abridgment, *Psychology: A Briefer Course* [1891]). What makes his work in this chapter so important is that James attacks full on the structuralist ("synthetic-method") approach to psychology, wherein we "start with sensations, as the simplest mental facts, and proceed synthetically, constructing each higher stage from those below it" (PP1, 224; WWJ, 21). However, such an approach, while arising from a traditional empirical philosophy, is inattentive to experience. As James says, "No one ever had a simple sensation by itself...what we call simple sensations are results of discriminative attention" (PP1, 224; WWJ, 21). The psychologist, James insists, only "has a right to postulate at the outset...that thinking of some sort goes on" (PP1, 224; WWJ, 21-22). This "first fact" leads James to posit that consciousness (of which thinking is a "state") is a stream, ever in flux and flow.

> Consciousness...does not appear to itself chopped up in bits. Such words as 'chain' or 'train' do not describe it fitly as it presents itself in the first instance. It is nothing jointed; it flows. A 'river' or a 'stream' are the metaphors by which it is most naturally described. (PP1, 239; WWJ, 33)

Thus, consciousness, even as early as the *Principles*, is no vessel, but a continuous stream in constant change and movement.

Eventually, James realized the need to abandon any vestiges of a substantive, metaphysical status for mind, and he began his disassembly just four years after the publication of the *Principles* in his presidential address to the American Psychological Association, "The Knowing of Things Together." In this piece, James, relying implicitly on the implications of his "stream of consciousness," argues that "knowing" is to know in the first instance collectively rather than individually. We do not, as "common sense" and "common psychology" suggest, "combine" or "bring things together" to make up a more complex experience (WWJ, 153). Even the very distinction between thought and thing breaks down when we turn our attention to experience in its immediacy. "The thought-stuff and the thing-stuff are here indistinguishably the same in nature" (WWJ, 156). The "ultimate datum," then, is "experience."

Finally, James is led to toss off altogether the remaining remnants of a substantive idea of consciousness. In his 1904 essay, "Does 'Consciousness' Exist?," he comes right out and says, "I believe that 'consciousness'…is on the point of disappearing altogether. It is the name of a nonentity, and has no right to a place among first principles" (WWJ, 169). Instead, consciousness, while not an entity, "does stand for a function [read: 'habit']…. That function is *knowing*" where "knowing can easily be explained as a particular sort of relation into which portions of pure experience may enter" (WWJ, 170). In lieu of the stream of consciousness, which must now be set aside, James relies solely on experience, "pure experience" to be specific. Thus, his new "metaphysic" becomes pure experience and his philosophical approach to experience he calls radical empiricism; it is to these psychologically informed concepts that we turn for the remainder of the chapter.

James's Radical Turn

James's first statement of radical empiricism comes in his introduction to his collection *The Will to Believe and Other Essays*. There he says:

> Were I obliged to give a short name to the *attitude* in question, I should call it that of radical empiricism, in spite of the fact that such brief nicknames are nowhere more misleading than in philosophy. I say 'empiricism,' because it is contented to regard its most assured conclusions concerning matters of fact as hypotheses liable to modification in the course of future experience; and I say 'radical,' because it treats the doctrine of monism itself as an hypothesis, and, unlike so much of the half-way empiricism that is current under the name of positivism and agnosticism or scientific naturalism, it does not dogmatically affirm monism as something with which all experience has got to square. (WWJ, 134 [emphasis added])

Initially, then, James speaks of radical empiricism as an "attitude," and further explains that it is an attitude that concerns the hypothetical nature of conclusive judgments that must respond to experience itself. Further, he claims that his is a "radical" take on empiricism because it eschews an underlying monism—that is, it does not believe that experience is ultimately reducible to one kind of thing, substance, or essence.

But why take such an attitude? James believes that such an attitude is necessary to combat what he calls "intellectualism" which "is the belief that our mind comes upon a world complete in itself and has the duty of ascertaining the world's contents; but has no power of re-determining its character, for that is already given" (WWJ, 735). Such a position, according to James, is deeply flawed. Both traditional "rationalists" and "empiricists" demonstrate a basic kind of intellectualism, demanding that "evidence" be had before belief (or "faith") is warranted. However, "It may be true that work is still doing in the world-process, and that in that work we are called to bear our share. The character of the world's results may in part depend upon our acts" (WWJ, 736).

Thus we see that James posits radical empiricism as the "melioristic" alternative to both traditional empiricism and rationalism. That is, he takes seriously both the empirical claim that we cannot know what tomorrow may bring and the belief that "a pluralistic universe's success...[requires] the good-will and active faith, theoretical as well as practical, of all concerned, to make it 'come true'" (WWJ, 737). But radical empiricism mediates more than just the philosophical debate between empiricists and rationalists. As early as his emotional crises of 1870, we see James begin to formulate a meliorist position that attempts to steer between the conflicting elements of his own life—the tug-of-war between "scientific" work and the "moral business" and between "hard facts" and "spiritual" matters. Thus, radical empiricism, though metaphysically pregnant, is ultimately a deep *human* psychological and philosophical *commitment* to two claims: (1) One must not deny anything that is experienced; and (2) One must not deny the potency of human action.

To deepen our understanding of these, we begin with a discussion of the first claim and will return to the second a bit later. However, it is important to see that for James, both claims necessarily hang together.

Committing to Experience

What exactly is meant by the notion that radical empiricism commits you to not denying experience? James's 1904 definition of this commitment may help:

> I give the name of 'radical empiricism' to my *Weltan-schauung* [world-view]. Empiricism is known as the opposite of rationalism. Rationalism tends to emphasize universals and to make wholes prior to parts in the order of logic as well as

that of being. Empiricism, on the contrary, lays the explanatory stress upon the part, the element, the individual, and treats the whole as a collection and the universal as an abstraction. My descriptions of things, accordingly, starts with the parts and makes of the whole a being of the second order. It is essentially a mosaic philosophy, a philosophy of plural facts, like that of Hume and his descendants, who refer these facts neither to Substances in which they inhere nor to an Absolute Mind that creates them as its objects. But it differs from the Humian type of empiricism in one particular which makes me add the epithet radical.

To be radical, an empiricism must neither admit into its constructions any element that is not directly experienced, nor exclude from them any element that is directly experienced. For such a philosophy, *the relations that connect experiences must themselves be experienced relations, and any kind of relation experienced must be accounted as 'real' as anything else in the system.* Elements may indeed by redistributed, the original placing of things getting corrected, but a real place must be found for every kind of thing experienced, whether term or relation, in the final philosophic arrangement. (WWJ, 195)

Let us put such a claim in psychological and philosophical context.

The history of Modern Western thought can be viewed as a debate between two metaphysical and epistemological positions. On the one hand rationalism, stemming from the work of Rene Descartes,[2] argues that the most basic stuff is spiritual or mental in nature, and that experience is the rational operation of a mind that is prior to and necessary for the possibility of experience. That is, ontologically (i.e., in order of "being"), mind is prior to experience. In contrast, empiricists believe that we have to start from experience itself. So, whereas Descartes argued that our perceptions only serve to implicate a mind that perceives, empiricists believe that perceptions tell us little if anything about what perceives, but about perceptions themselves. This is most evident in the philosophy of David Hume (1711-1776) whose empiricism takes a skeptical turn on the very possibility of the perceiving self. In fact, for Hume perceptions are so discrete that even the acceptance of causal relations is a "fiction" of the imagination. The most that we can say about how (or if) our impressions hang together is that there seems to be a relation of "constant conjunction" for some parts of our experience.[3] This take on experience, a direct outcome of the path begun by John Locke (1632-1704) and carried forth by George Berkeley (1685-1753), had uncomfortable consequences for many philosophers. In particular, it was this form of empiricism that awoke Immanuel Kant (1724-1804) from his "dogmatic slumbers," resulting in Kant's positing (once again) that there must be something prior to experience in order to hold experience together. That is, since we do, in fact, experience the connections among our impressions, there must be some apparatus that makes such experience possible. For Kant, this was transcendental ego, or mind. From Kant's philosophy, there followed decades of so-called "idealists" (e.g., Fichte and Hegel in Germany, Bradley and Greene in England, and Royce in America). The idealists slowly stripped away any pretense of any reality separate from the ideas found in the mind.

Jamesian radical empiricism is an attempt to avoid pitfalls he saw in both the rationalists and idealists on one side and the traditional empiricists on the other. In particular, James insists, like the empiricists before him, that experience is all we have and that no ability to "get behind" or "beyond" experience is possible. As such, we can only start from experience as we find it—namely, in its rich plurality. But unlike traditional empiricists who believe that experience reduces to atomic sensations and deny the experience of relations themselves, James requires that a commitment to radical empiricism be a commitment to all that is experienced. For James this demands that we recognize as "real" any *experienced* relation. As he says, "Radical empiricism…is fair to both the unity and the disconnection. It finds no reason for treating either as illusory" (WWJ, 197). Such a commitment, then, not only undermines atomic empiricism, it need not rely on a transcendental metaphysic either since relations as part of experience need no extra-experiential apparatus to support them. "*Radical empiricism*, as I understand it, *does full justice to…relations*, without, however, treating them as rationalism always tends to treat them, as being true in some supernal way" (WWJ, 196).

Another definitive discussion of "radical empiricism" solidifies our account.

> Radical empiricism consists first of a postulate, next a statement of fact, and finally of a general conclusion.
>
> The postulate is that the only things that shall be debatable among philosophers shall be things definable in terms drawn from experience. [Things of an unexperienceable na-

ture may exist ad libitum, but they form no part of the material for philosophical debate.]

The statement of fact is that the relations between things, conjunctive as well as disjunctive, are just as much matters of direct particular experience, neither more so nor less so, than the things themselves.

The generalized conclusion is that therefore the parts of experience hold together from next to next by relations that are themselves parts of experience. The directly apprehended universe needs, in short, no extraneous trans-empirical connective support, but posses in its own right a concatenated or continuous structure. (WWJ, 136)

James *postulates* that *only and all* experience matters to philosophy—James's radical empiricism establishes an attitude, an approach to philosophy writ-large. Once such a vision of philosophy is postulated, a "fact" about experience itself is put forth—namely, the "parts" of experience include both "disjunctive" *and* "conjunctive" elements, and this "fact" leads to the "conclusion" that while experience is individuateable, it is also constitutively self-supporting *in and through* its content. Ours, accordingly, is a "pluralistic universe," but rather than merely consisting of atomic sensations (as Hume argued), James claims this plurality includes the connections among sensations as well.

The concrete pulses of experience appear pent in by no such definite limits as our conceptual substitutes for them are confined by. They run into one another continuously and seem to interpenetrate.... You feel no one of them as inwardly simple, and no two as wholly without confluence where they touch. There is no datum so small as not to show this mystery, if mystery it be. (WWJ, 294)

Unfortunately, this use of language by James can be misleading, for such ways of speaking imply an already existing agent who "feels" and "experiences." But it is important to note that, in fact, radical empiricism admits of no such dichotomy a priori.

Experience, I believe, has no such inner duplicity; and the separation of it into consciousness and content comes, not by way of subtraction, but by way of addition—the addition, to the given concrete piece of it, of other sets of experiences. (WWJ, 172)

Delineation of "agent" and "object" in experience requires the *addition* of other experiences, and that addition is determined by purpose. "There is no thought-stuff different from thing-stuff.... [S]ubjectivity and objectivity are affairs not of what an experience is aboriginally made of, but of its classification. Classifications depend on temporary purposes." (WWJ, 271-272).

A World Purely of Experience

James first posits this approach to experience in his chapter from *The Principles of Psychology*, "The Steam of Thought" (PP1, 224-290; WWJ, 21-74). AS mentioned earlier, therein James notes that thought, like a stream, flows without differentiation. Within the stream itself, features are not observable without the presence of some interruption. Interruption or disruption constitutes a unique moment where purpose takes over in order to enable the stream to continue its flow. But like a stream interrupted by rock-formations, a transaction occurs within experience wherein the interruption alters the direction of the current while the current wears into the disruption. Neither continues unscathed in the process.

In what James calls a "world of pure experience" plurality abounds, but it abounds in an undifferentiated way. Differentiation is an experienced, functional act which arises out of the flow of experience itself as a way to control the quasi-chaos long enough to accomplish things. James uses the unfortunate adjective "pure" to describe undifferentiated experience and further undermines his metaphysics with slipshod language. The betrayal of his language comes in the form of positing a state wherein there is only "pure" experience—what some commentators have called the "really real" for James. However, it would be a mistake to read James in this way. Too much in his work speaks against such a reading.

James has deep concern for the metaphysical problem he calls the conflict between "the one and the many," sometimes choosing to call it the conflict between monism and pluralism. "Pure" experience read as the "really real" implies a monistic metaphysics, but James never comes down on the side of "the one" in his discussions. His own comments suggest that "pure" experience is more metaphorical, a philosophical device to shift metaphysical perspective. As such it is instrumental to his philosophy, not fundamental. Radical empiricism only demands that we take experience seriously as the source and content of philosophy, it does not posit—even explicitly eschews—a priori what experience is. Experience,

29

for James, admits of infinite possibility, thus it admits of infinite plurality. It is not one thing that mutates, but infinite undifferentiated somethings.

Experience is also importantly organic. As James tells us, experience grows; and in particular, it grows "by its edges" (WWJ, 212). The center of the stream carries water come what may, but the bottom and sides wear away the soil, shifting the landscape. James's philosophy of experience is, thereby conservative. The world, though historically contingent and malleable, is neither arbitrary nor capricious. By growing "by its edges," it protects the center from catastrophic disruption in most cases. What James says in the context of a discussion of "habit" could easily be said of experience itself: "[It is] weak enough to yield to influence, but strong enough not to yield all at once" (WWJ, 10).

A radical empiricist stance that sees all and only experience helps solve an epistemological concern as well. In a world of "pure experience" no division of knower and known can be made without referenced to experience itself. Traditional rationalism and empiricism posit a necessary divide between knower and known such that the knower is an entity that stands outside experience itself and is said to "have" experience that is either true or false about that which is known. We will say more about this in the next chapter, but as we have already mentioned James states that experience has no such "inner duplicity." The "consciousness," posited by previous philosophies as an entity that thinks and knows, is for James a function of experience itself. So the knower, on James's account, functions as that part of experience which sets an investigation into motion, and the known is that in which the investigation culminates. When we look at experience carved up for epistemological reasons, what we find is a point where something generates an investigation that is pursued to its end. "[The] starting-point…becomes a knower and [the] terminus and object meant or known" (WWJ, 201; original in italics). Note that all this is explainable on experiential terms (but only when we take the radically empirical position that connections are part and parcel of experience) *and* that such determination of knower and known can only be made upon reflection into otherwise undifferentiated experience. It is *all there*, richly, deeply, pluralistically—but each differentiation must be taken functionally, not fundamentally.

As we noted earlier, what James could only imply in his 1890 *Principles*, he stated explicitly 10 years later in a famous essay "Does 'Consciousness' Exist?" (WWJ, 169-183): psychology is about experience and consciousness as a function therein, not about some entity called consciousness which functions to provide experience. It is not about the functions *of* the mind but about mind *as* function. Philosophy, as concerned with experience, supercedes psychology, and further, as radically empirical, philosophy makes no specific contentions about experience; it is first and foremost visionary, not disciplinary.

Taken as visionary, radical empiricism is a metaphilosophical agenda rather than a theory of experience—radical empiricism sets the agenda for philosophy, it tries to keep philosophy honest. James's own inner conflicts with science and religion demonstrate this point as he uses radical empiricism to resolve this important conflict. Science taken too far denies human potency (insofar as it is deterministic, for example); religion taken too far requires a retreat from experience (insofar as it requires that one deny that there is evil and risk, for example). James saw that both positions are psychologically paralyzing: A person can commit fully and exclusively to either science or religion *only* by resolving to stop thinking, or, as we shall see below, in a more Jamesian tone, "stop living."

Returning to Life

Experience "breaks" along functional, not ontological lines. That is, to carve up experience into specific experiences, even into experiencer and experiences, is ontologically unwarranted. Emphatically, James says, "The only function one experience can perform is to lead into another experience; and the only fulfillment we can speak of is the reaching of a certain experienced end" (WWJ, 203). Experiences serve a function, namely to lead to further experience. To control the quasi-chaotic flow of pluralistic experience, reason is employed, but in order to meet James's own conditions, reason itself must be describable in experiential terms.

For James, then, rational reflection functions as experience employed in response to breaks in the flow of experience. Reason attempts to "fit" such breaks back into the flow, to "make sense of" or "give meaning to" otherwise discontinuously experienced elements of experience. But though influenced by Charles Peirce's pragmatic philosophy (see the next chapter), James's take on this process is much more psychological than the logically inclined Peirce before him. When Peirce posited his notion of an "irritation of doubt" (5.358-387), such doubt began a logical project. For James, however, such disruption is discussed in primarily psychological terms:

31

> Any unobstructed tendency to action discharges itself without
> the production of much cogitative accompaniment, and any
> perfectly fluent course of thought awakens but little feeling;
> but when the movement is inhibited, or when the thought
> meets with difficulties, we experience distress. (WWJ, 318)

The cures for such distresses are the processes of reason, of inquiry.
We develop concepts that we, in turn, employ in order to control the
chaos. However,

> The essence of life is its continuously changing character; but
> our concepts are all discontinuous and fixed, and the only
> mode of making them coincide with life is by arbitrarily sup-
> posing positions of arrest therein.... When we conceptualize,
> we cut out and fix, and exclude everything but what we have
> fixed. (WWJ, 573-574)

Thus, our very solutions lose touch with experience, with life itself,
for life is neither neat nor clear. James's philosophy wants us to taste life
as it is, and plumb its depths and darkest corners. "It is, in short, a reinstatement of the vague to its proper place in our mental life which I am
so anxious to press on the attention" (WWJ, 45).

Intellectualizing, the use of mere words, of idle speculation, of logical analysis, carves up experience into palatable packages, but it also ar-
rests the flow of experience and masks the underlying tensions of living.
However, we are always *in media res*, and this fact alone places us beyond a space of mere intellectual speculation without context or action.
James insists that experience, his own "radical empiricism," and, for that
matter, philosophy itself demand connection to human activity, pursuit,
even courage. Mere speculation, bare theory, simple words, which
ground much of so-called "intellectualism," cannot meet the conditions of
human living. "As long as one continues *talking*, intellectualism remains
in undisturbed possession of the field. The return to life can't come about
by talking. It is an *act*" (WWJ, 297).

The desired end of reason is best understood not logically but phe-
nomenologically:

> Th[e] feeling of the sufficiency of the present moment, of its
> absoluteness,—this absence of all need to explain it, account
> for it, or justify it,—is what I call the Sentiment of Rationality.
> (WWJ, 318)

Taking Philosophy Personally

Actions in the face of problems return us to life, and these actions are "resolute" when experience is absent of the need to explain itself, when we return to ever-flowing experience.

* * *

Our discussions in this chapter demonstrate that, ultimately, radical empiricism is best understood not as philosophical doctrine, but as philosophical vision. It is our contention that this view makes radical empiricism contiguous with James's own life—a quasi-chaos of confusing elements, now monistic, now pluralistic, at once both elite and democratic, stable and precarious, malleable and firm, righteous and ignoble. Radical empiricism takes these seemingly contradictory aspects of life in stride for experience itself has "no such inner duplicity." This is both psychologically frustrating and philosophically interesting. For life, then, becomes what we make it. Meaning is in the many and multiple meanings which arise from the great variety of ideals we posit and the various means we can conjure up in pursuit of them. As we shall see, James's radically empirical world demands much of us, morally and spiritually. It demands a "strenuous mood," vigilance, and fortitude if progress in life is to be gained. We cannot rely on any transcendent being, though belief in such a being may help us act more urgently. James has no metaphysical principle in which to find solace. Experience is all there is, and we must make of it what we can. How to choose in what directions we might go?—that is the stuff of the rest of this study.

Endnotes

[1] Josiah Royce, *William James and Other Essays on the Philosophy of Life* (New York: Macmillan, 1911), 7.

[2] Cf. Rene Descartes, *Meditations on First Philosophy*, and for a discussion of Cartesian philosophy see Garret Thomson, *On Descartes* (Belmont, CA: Wadsworth, 2000).

[3] Cf., David Hume, *A Treatise of Human Nature*. Selby-Bigge and Nidditch edition (Oxford: Oxford University Press, 1978). For a discussion of Humean philosophy, see Elizabeth Radcliffe, *On Hume* (Belmont, CA: Wadsworth, 2000).

33

3

Philosophy in Action: William James and Pragmatism

*Philosophies, whether expressed in sonnets or systems, all
must wear this form. The thinker starts from some experience
of the practical world, and asks its meaning. He launches
himself upon the speculative sea, and makes a voyage long or
short. He ascends into the empyrean, and communes with the
eternal essences. But whatever his achievements and discov-
eries be while gone, the utmost result they can issue in is some
new practical maxim or resolve, or the denial of some old one,
with which inevitably he is sooner or later washed ashore on
the* terra firma *of concrete life again.*

—"Reflex Action and Theism" (WTB, 142-143)

In the preceding chapter, we emphasized the urgency in James's philosophical work; according to James, philosophical reflection is *not* an
optional activity, but a psychological, human, necessity. Indeed James
sometimes refers to philosophical thinking as a natural kind of "craving"
(WTB 82)—we long for order, rationality, security, and system within a
"restless universe" (WWJ, 606) of irreducibly plural facts, fluctuation,

exuberance, risk, joy, tragedy, and loss. James argues that the primary mission of a radically empirical philosophy is to reconcile us to our condition, to make us feel at home in the universe. Yet if a philosophy is to do this, it must take full account of the kind of universe we are living in as well as of the kind of creatures we are. That is, as we argued earlier, the radical empiricist holds that if a philosophy is to be successful, it must satisfy two criteria: First, it must not deny or contradict any of the facts of lived experience; it must not depart from life. Second, it must not deny the power of human action to effect changes in the universe; it must not obstruct or paralyze human effort. Hence a radically empirical philosophy will directly confront the flux and flow of life in "all its wild intensity" (WWJ, 648) and yet assure each of us that "the inmost nature of the reality is congenial to the powers which you possess" (WWJ, 331). James argued that traditional philosophical systems failed to meet the criteria of radical empiricism, and that hence a new philosophy was needed.

To this end, in 1907 James published one of the most controversial works of twentieth-century philosophy, *Pragmatism: A New Name for Some Old Ways of Thinking*. In this slim book, which originated in a series of lectures James gave at the Lowell Institute in 1906 and at Columbia University in 1907, drew upon the previous work of his close friend, Charles Sanders Peirce (1839-1914) and popularized "pragmatism," the first philosophical movement indigenous to the United States. It is a discussion of James's pragmatism that forms the subject of the present chapter; however, before we can begin, we must turn first to Peirce's account out of which James develops his own views.

The Origins of Pragmatism

James credits Peirce with originating the term 'pragmatism' and its leading principle, the "pragmatic maxim."[1] Peirce proposed the principal tenets of pragmatism at the meetings of an informal philosophy group that met in Cambridge, Massachusetts in the early 1870s, and the group called itself the "Metaphysical Club" (recall our discussion from the previous chapter).[2] Drawing upon their discussions, Peirce wrote two essays, "The Fixation of Belief" (5.358-387) and "How to Make Our Ideas Clear" (5.388-410), which mark the birth of pragmatism.[3]

Peirce's "Fixation" and "Ideas" articles are today considered among the most important in philosophy; however, at the time of their publication they received little notice. The groundwork of pragmatism lay dormant for some 20 years until James made use of Peirce's ideas in an 1898 address entitled "Philosophical Conceptions and Practical Results." In this essay, James credits Peirce with first proposing the "principle of pragmatism" which James confesses "should be expressed more broadly than Mr. Peirce expresses it" (WWJ, 348). However, to understand James's reconstruction of Peirce's concept, we must examine briefly the leading ideas of Peircean pragmatism.

Peirce and the Pragmatic Maxim

The essence of Peirce's pragmatism lies in the principle of meaning, commonly known as the 'pragmatic maxim', first expressed in "How to Make Our Ideas Clear." However, this principle is based upon the theory of belief launched in the earlier "Fixation of Belief" article, so it is to Peirce's concept of belief that we must first turn.

In "Fixation" Peirce addresses a seemingly simple question: What does it mean to have a *belief*? According to many philosophers, to have a belief is to be in a certain psychological state with regard to a given statement or idea. That is, to believe that *snow is white* is to adopt a certain psychological attitude—one of affirmation—towards the statement, 'snow is white'. On the traditional analysis, then, belief is essentially a psychological phenomenon; beliefs are inner, mental, and private. They are, consequently, inaccessible to another person's observation—one cannot tell what your beliefs are just by *looking* at you—and hence not subject to scientific examination.

Contrary to Modern philosophical tradition, however, Peirce sought to rid philosophy of the notion of an "inner" consciousness inherited from the influential French philosopher, Rene Descartes.[4] Wanting to set philosophy on more "scientific" ground, Peirce proposed a theory of belief according to which beliefs are not essentially mental states, but rather *rules for action*, or as Peirce would say "habits" (5.371).[5] On the Peircean analysis, to believe that *this knife is sharp* is to be disposed to *behave* in certain ways when presented with the knife. Put more generally, to have a belief is simply to have acquired a habit of acting in certain ways under certain conditions. This take on beliefs as, in essence, habits entails that they are not inner and private, but publicly observable. But how does a belief lead to active habitual expressions of it?

Peirce answers in this way: the public action that expresses belief is a function of the *meaning* of the idea or statement to which the belief refers. That is, the belief that *this knife is sharp* will generate certain behavior depending upon the meaning of the idea 'this knife is sharp'. Therefore, Peirce's theory of belief requires a theory of meaning, and it is in "How to Make Our Ideas Clear" that Peirce gives the first articulation of the "pragmatic maxim" by which one discerns the meaning of an idea:

> Consider what effects, that might conceivably have practical bearings, we conceive the object of our conception to have. Then our conception of these effects is the whole of our conception of the object. (5.402)

Here, again, we find Peirce resisting the traditional tendency. Not unlike the concept of a "belief," the concept of "meaning" has been understood in traditional philosophy to be primarily a psychological property, but on Peirce's view, the meaning of an idea is to be analyzed in terms of the effects of its object in a person's experience. "Meaning," like "belief," is thus taken out of the realm of private consciousness and placed into the world of action and behavior.

To gain a better understanding of Peirce's maxim, let us see how it is applied. When someone says of an object, X, that it is 'hard' what does she mean?[6] On Peirce's view, "our idea of anything is our idea of its sensible effects" (5.401); therefore, one can mean by the term 'hard', for example, only some set of sensory experiences. According to Peirce, to say that something is hard is to say that it will scratch other objects. Therefore, to say that 'X is hard' is to say X will scratch other objects. To emphasize the behavioral aspect of Peirce's theory, we may, alternatively, state this meaning in the form of an if-then sentence (in logic, such statements are called "conditionals"). Taken this way, the statement 'X is hard' means:

> *If you rub X against another object, Y, then X will scratch Y.*

Returning, then, to the statement 'the knife is sharp', the term 'sharp' means some collection of sensible effects—namely, to say that something is sharp is to say that it will cut other objects. Hence the statement, 'the knife is sharp' means something like the conditional:

> *If you draw the knife across the surface of another object, the knife will cut it.*

As these examples illustrate, meaning for Peirce is brought down to "what is tangible and conceivably practical" (5.400); the meaning of a term consists in the "sensible effects" it predicates of an object, and the meaning of a statement is essentially a proposal, or perhaps a prediction, regarding the functioning of its object. For any idea, then, one may extract its complete meaning by drawing out the proposals for action that it suggests:

> If one can identify accurately all the conceivable phenomena which the affirmation or denial of a concept could imply, one will have therein a complete definition of the concept, *and there is absolutely nothing more in it.* (5.412)

Indeed, Peirce thought that drawn-out proposals were *exhaustive* of an idea's meaning.

With Peirce's theory of meaning in place, let us return to the concept of belief. To have the belief that *this knife is sharp* is to be disposed to act in accordance with the various proposals that constitute the meaning of the statement 'this knife is sharp'. One who believes *this knife is sharp* is likely to exhibit certain kinds of behavior in the presence of the knife: she will avoid contact with the blade, she will not use the knife as a back scratcher, she will store it in a place that children cannot easily access, she will apply it to those object he wishes to cut, etc. It is important to recognize that Peirce is not claiming that the belief that *this knife is sharp* is the *cause* of the various kinds of behavior, for this would be to admit that a belief is a psychological state that is separate from behavior. Rather, Peirce is arguing that believing *consists* in the behavioral dispositions; a belief *is* a habit.

In Peirce's later writings on the topic, one discovers that principle of meaning expressed by the pragmatic maxim is all he intended to denote with the term 'pragmatism'. In a 1905 manuscript, Peirce writes:

> Suffice it to say once more that pragmatism is, in itself, no doctrine of metaphysics, no attempt to determine any truth of things. It is merely a method of ascertaining the meanings of hard words and of abstract concepts. (5.464)

Thus, on Peirce's view, pragmatism is not a philosophy *per se*, it is rather a logical rule to employ when doing philosophy. This rule is supposed to help philosophers "dismiss" the "make-believes" (5.416) of previous philosophizing. That is, the pragmatic maxim is intended to be used as a weapon against the imprecise and vague vocabulary of traditional philosophy.

To see that this is so, consider the following: Insofar as the maxim proposes a standard of meaning, it also establishes a criterion of *meaninglessness*. Since the meaning of a term consists in the sensible effects it predicates of its object, and the meaning of a statement or idea consists in the functional proposals it makes to an agent, any term that cannot be defined with reference to sensory experience, and any statement that makes no proposal to action will be without meaning.

Peirce thought that many philosophical ideas, and the disputes concerning them, were meaningless and should be therefore abandoned. Take, for example, the old metaphysical dilemma of free will. Those who believe in free will, "libertarians," maintain that one's actions are the expression of the free choice of one's will. Their opponents, "determinists," maintain that one's actions are the necessary effects of the causal force of prior events, and therefore that the will is not free.[7] According to the pragmatic maxim, the meaning of an idea consists in the proposals it makes to action. Does either position make such a proposal? It seems that the answer is no—behavior is unaffected no matter how the free will question is answered. The competing claims are therefore meaningless, and the dispute between them is idle. As with the free will debate, so with traditional metaphysics in general:

> [Pragmatism] will serve to show that almost every proposition of ontological metaphysics is either meaningless gibberish— one word being defined by other words, and they by still others, without any real conception ever being reached—or else downright absurd. (5.423)

Peirce imagined a time at which, through the application of his maxim, philosophy would be purged of all nonsense. At this time, all that would remain is "a series of problems capable of investigation by the observational methods of the true sciences" (5.423).

James's Pragmatism

Peirce's emphasis on science may generate some concern. For example, can statements about values meet the criterion for meaningfulness established by the pragmatic maxim? Will statements such as *murder is wrong* and *Beethoven is a better composer than Mozart* be meaningful on a Peircean analysis? How can concerns about decidedly human matters such as how we should live and what is valuable fit into Peirce's scientific world-view? Most generally, can Peircean pragmatism meet the requirements of a radically empirical approach to philosophy? On the face of it, the answer would seem "no." Peirce's pragmatic maxim seems to remove from the arena of philosophical concern the kinds of topics that James thought most vital and with which he was most eager to struggle; in this sense Peircean pragmatism is not radically empirical. James hence saw the need to develop a more elastic and human version of pragmatism.

Philosophy's "Present Dilemma"

In his *Pragmatism* lectures, James begins working towards the development of his more human version in the first lecture entitled "The Present Dilemma in Philosophy." Therein, James argues that professional philosophy is caught in the deadlock of two opposing viewpoints: rationalism and empiricism. These philosophies are, in turn, the intellectual manifestations of two opposing psychological types or, as James calls them, "temperaments": the "tender mind" and the "tough mind." The tender-minded, rationalist philosopher is devoted to "abstract and eternal principles" (WWJ, 364); he is religious, optimistic, and spiritual. According to the tender-minded philosopher, the universe exists as a complete, simple, and rational whole. Accordingly, tender-minded philosophies tend to dismiss the flux, struggle, and risk of life as merely apparent and unreal.

The tender-minded temperament is perhaps most clearly evident in one of James's favorite targets, the German philosopher, G. W. F. Hegel (1770-1831), who is famous for having maintained that "what is rational is actual and what is actual is rational."[8] On the Hegelian view, all conflicts and fluctuations are but temporary moments in the self-realization of an already immanent Absolute Reality that Hegel called *Geist* ("Spirit").[9] Hence the travails and struggles of human life are in reality transitory and predestined to resolve in the final culmination of an Absolute. There is thus no *risk* in the Hegelian universe; the final salvation of the world is inevitable and *guaranteed.* Against this kind of optimism, James asserts his radical empiricism,

> I find myself willing to take the universe to be really dangerous and adventurous, without therefore backing out and crying 'no play'.... I am willing that there should be real losses and real losers, and no total preservation of all that is. (WWJ, 470)

By contrast, the tough-minded empiricist is committed to "facts in all their crude variety"; he is scientific, skeptical, and materialistic (WWJ, 364). The tough-minded thinker naturally rejects the optimism of the tender-minded philosophies, he sees the world not as a rational whole, but as a sundry collection of the kinds of hard facts uncovered by science. As such, tough-minded philosophies tend to be pessimistic, irreligious, and fatalistic (WWJ, 365).

We have already seen some of James's criticisms of tough-minded empiricism in our discussion of radical empiricism from the preceding chapter. Recall that James rejects the *sensationalism* of traditional empiricism; that is, he rejects the idea that experience is analyzable into discreet, atomic sensations. Against this view, James promotes the idea that experience is primarily a stream, a flow of life that features both *disjunctive* and *conjunctive* relations; accordingly, the tough-minded empiricist's distinct, atomic sensations are not the ultimate elements of analysis. On James's view, experience is "all shades and no boundaries" (WWJ, 296)

Here James adds to this criticism the charge that tough-minded philosophies are not *living* philosophies; their commitment to the hard facts of science causes them to disregard the human features of experience. Consequently, a tough-minded philosophy cannot "return to life," it cannot keep in touch with the ordeals of lived experience, and so must detach itself. The Scottish empiricist, David Hume, provides a clear example of this tendency. Hume's *Treatise of Human Nature* is a paradigmatic example of tough-minded empiricism.[10] In his *Treatise*, Hume argues against the reality of causal relations and against the reality of a unified self that exists over time. To employ the Jamesian terminology, Hume recognizes only the *disjunctions* within experience, and dismisses the *conjunctions*. Hume hence resigns himself to a certain kind of skepticism; that is, he rejects the idea that real knowledge can be attained.

Hume is most famous for his skepticism, and many have taken his skeptical conclusions to be sufficient reason for abandoning his philosophy. However, James sees another target. In a telling passage from conclusion of the first book of his *Treatise*, Hume offers the following commentary:

> Most fortunately it happens, that since reason is incapable of dispelling these clouds, nature herself suffices to that purpose, and cures me of this philosophical melancholy and delirium.... I dine, I play a game of back-gammon, I converse, and am merry with my friends; and when after three or four hour's amusement, I would return to these speculations, they appear so cold, and strained, and ridiculous, that I cannot find in my heart to enter into them any further.[11]

Here Hume confesses that his philosophy must be abandoned once he leaves his study. Indeed, he goes further by claiming that he is led by "nature herself" to abandon the "melancholy and delirium" generated by his philosophical ideas; his nature compels him to *live*, and he can do so only by disregarding his philosophical principles. According to James's radically empirical view, Hume's admission constitutes a *refutation* of his philosophy.[12]

So, herein lies philosophy's dilemma: traditional systems offer one or the other of a pair of errors. The tough-minded philosophies offer "inhumanism" and "irreligion" whereas the tender-minded systems keep "out of all definite touch with concrete facts and joys and sorrows" (WWJ, 368); in other words, Western philosophical tradition leaves you with "an empirical philosophy that is not religious enough, and a religious philosophy that is not empirical enough" (WWJ, 367). James insists that no one can *live* without both the facts of the tough-minded philosophers and the principles of the tender-minded (WWJ, 364). Hence the traditional philosophical enterprise, conducted as it is on the model of the dilemma between rationalism and empiricism, is a strictly academic exercise, unfit to speak to the concerns of everyday life. In this connection, James quotes a student of his who remarked, "when you entered a philosophic classroom you had to open relations with a universe entirely distinct from the one you left behind you in the street" (WWJ, 369). In contrast to this image of philosophy, James asserts:

> The whole function of philosophy ought to be to find out what difference it will make to you and me, at definite instants of our life, if this world-formula or that world-formula be the one which is true. (WWJ, 379)

That is, a philosophy, if it is to perform a function at all, must begin with our actual hopes and needs, it must take seriously our pre-philosophical "temperaments," for these "do determine men in their philosophies, and always will" (WWJ, 374). Once these are accounted for, James insists we will find that,

> You want a system that will combine both things, the scientific loyalty to facts and willingness to take account of them, the spirit of adaptation and accommodation, in short, but also the old confidence in human values and the resultant spontaneity, whether of the religious or romantic type. (WWJ, 368)

42

James sought to develop a new philosophy that would mitigate the intellectual deadlock between the tender-minded and the tough-minded by accommodating the best aspects of each. He hoped that such a perspective would be able to bring philosophy back into touch with the daily lives of ordinary people. According to James, pragmatism is such a philosophy:

> I offer you the oddly-named thing pragmatism as a philosophy that can satisfy both kinds of demand. It can remain religious like the rationalisms, but at the same time, like the empiricisms, it can preserve the richest intimacy with facts. (WWJ, 373)

The Pragmatic Method

We can already begin to see that unlike Peirce, who thought that pragmatism would expose the meaninglessness of most metaphysical disputes, James claims that pragmatism is "primarily a method of settling metaphysical disputes that otherwise might be interminable" (WWJ, 377). That is, whereas Peirce specifically delimits pragmatism's scope, attempting to eschew metaphysics itself, James clearly presents his version of pragmatism as a "philosophy," a way to handle, not avoid, metaphysics. Despite this change in focus, James's method is, in essence, just a broadened version of Peirce's pragmatic maxim. James writes in his earlier essay, "Philosophical Conceptions and Practical Results":

> If there were any part of a thought that made no difference in the thought's practical consequences, then that part would be no proper element of the thought's significance. (WWJ, 348)

In the 1907 Pragmatism lectures, he explains the method thus:

> To attain perfect clearness in our thoughts of an object...we need only consider what effects of a conceivably practical kind the object may involve—what sensations we are to expect from it, and what actions we must prepare. Our conception of these effects, then, is for us the whole of our conception of the object, so far as that conception has positive significance at all. (WWJ, 377-378)

It would seem, thus far, that James has done nothing more than paraphrase Peirce. Like Peirce, James locates the meaning of an idea within its "practical consequences" for behavior. We begin to see the novel element in James's formulation, however, upon examination of the notion of a "practical consequence."

Whereas Peirce, as we saw above, limits the practical consequences of an idea to those functional proposals which it predicates of its object, James designs his pragmatism to include within a given idea's pragmatic meaning its implications for the *entirety* of the believing subject's experience. James realizes that belief in certain philosophical doctrines can be *paralyzing*, that certain philosophical doctrines can induce attitudes that *obstruct* action and literally *stifle* the flow of life. James argues that such consequences, which may be characterized as "psychological," are certainly *practical*, they most definitely affect our behavior, and a pragmatism that is radically empirical must account for them. That is, Jamesian pragmatism "plunges forward into the river of experience" (WWJ, 405), and attempts to confront it whole.

Resolution, then, and not necessarily dissolution, is the purpose of James's pragmatism, for James saw more clearly than Peirce that metaphysical disputes can enervate, disrupting our activities. However, as we have said, James's pragmatic method to take on such crippling disputes is contiguous with Peirce's own maxim. James says:

> The pragmatic method in...cases [of dispute] is to try to interpret each notion by tracing its respective practical consequences. What difference would it practically make to anyone if this notion rather than that notion were true? If no practical difference whatever can be traced, then the alternatives mean practically the same thing, and all dispute is idle. (WWJ, 377)

One way to get inside the important changes that James makes to Peirce's doctrine, however, is through his own discussion of the debate between materialism and spiritualism (WWJ, 393ff.). Traditionally, materialism is the position that maintains that only matter, and the laws of physics that govern it, exists. Further, while matter of some sort may always exist, the laws of physical nature imply that the world as we know it will dissolve away. Consequently, materialists deny the existence of spiritual entities such as souls, minds, and God, as well as the ideas of immortality and eternity. Alternatively, spiritualism claims that there is more to the universe than just blind matter. There is in addition another kind of substance—"spirit"—which is eternal, and eternal things are superior to finite entities; thus "spirit" is superior to matter thus superior to matter.

Philosophy in Action

Of course, the dispute between materialists and spiritualists cannot be resolved by means of observation. The competing claims cannot be analyzed into claims about sense experience; evidence is inconclusive. We must then apply the pragmatic method "by tracing its respective practical consequences." In so doing, an immediate implication of James's method when applied to the spiritualism-materialism debate comes into strict relief: if we were to imagine ourselves living at the very last moment of the universe's existence, the dispute between materialism and spiritualism is idle. That is, if there literally were *no future* in which pragmatic differences in behavior and attitude could manifest, "the two theories, in spite of their different-sounding names, mean exactly the same thing" (WWJ, 395). As James puts the point elsewhere,

> There can *be* no difference anywhere that doesn't *make* a difference elsewhere—no difference in abstract truth that doesn't express itself in a difference in concrete fact and in conduct consequent upon that fact, imposed on somebody, somehow, somewhere, and somewhen. (WWJ, 379)

James hence insists that in "every genuine metaphysical debate some practical issue, however conjectural and remote, is involved" (WWJ, 396); where no practical issue can be identified, debate is "purely verbal" (WWJ, 395) and consequently may be simply dismissed.

Yet as this is not very last moment of the universe's existence (we hope), the dispute between materialism and spiritualism *does* matter. Applying this method to the competing claims in the debate, James shows that there is a significant difference between the materialist thesis and that of the spiritualist. Taken pragmatically, the materialist position amounts to the claim:

> In the vast driftings of the cosmic weather, though many a jeweled shore appears and many an enchanted cloud-bank floats away, long lingering ere it be dissolved—even as our world now lingers, for our joy—yet when these transient products are gone, nothing, absolutely *nothing* remains, to represent those particular qualities, those elements of preciousness which they may have enshrined. Dead and gone are they, gone utterly from the very sphere and room of being. Without an echo; without a memory... (WWJ, 397-398)

The spiritualist, on the other hand, is pragmatically committed to the following assertion:

45

On James

> A world with a God in it to say the last word, may indeed burn
> up or freeze, but we then think of him as still mindful of the
> old ideals and sure to bring them elsewhere to fruition; so that,
> where he is, tragedy is only provisional and partial, and ship
> wreck and dissolution not the absolutely final things. (WWJ,
> 398)

James intentionally employs dramatic language in characterizing the
competing positions because he wants us to feel the *gravity* of the dispute
for our own lives. Taken pragmatically, the debate between materialism
and spiritualism is no longer simply a matter of interest to the detached
speculation of academic philosophers, it is rather an issue which cuts to
the very core of *how we shall live.* James summarizes the debate:

> Here then, in these different emotional and practical appeals,
> in these adjustments of our concrete attitudes of hope and ex-
> pectation, and all the delicate consequences which their differ-
> ences entail, lie the real meanings of materialism and [spiritu-
> alism]—not in hair-splitting abstractions.... Materialism
> means simply the denial that the moral order is eternal, and
> the shutting off of ultimate hopes; [spiritualism] means the af-
> firmation of an eternal moral order and the letting loose of
> hope. (WWJ, 398)

The metaphysician's sterile question regarding the existence of spiritual
entities thus becomes on a radically empirical analysis a question of our
own psychological attitude towards the universe: Shall we sustain *hope*
for the universe, or shall we abandon hope? Certainly, we shall have to
adopt one or the other of these attitudes—suspending judgment on the
matter is to suspend hope. We must choose, and how we choose will sig-
nificantly impact our behavior. What shall we do?

Understood pragmatically, the dispute is easily resolved. The "true
objection to materialism" does not lie in some intricate philosophical argument, it lies in the realization that materialism does not provide a "permanent warrant for our more ideal interests"; it is not a "fulfiller of our
remotest hopes"; it results in "utter final wreck and tragedy" (WWJ, 398).
Spiritualism, by contrast, "has at least this practical superiority... it guar-
antees an ideal order that shall be permanently preserved," it "takes our
joyous, careless, trustful moments, and it justifies them" (WWJ, 398).
The need to believe in an "eternal moral order" is "one of the deepest
needs of our breast" (WWJ, 389). Whereas "materialism's sun sets in a

46

sea of disappointment" (WWJ, 399), spiritualism "deals with a world of *promise*" and is, thus, pragmatically justified.

The Jamesian strategy for dealing with metaphysical disputes, then, is to translate the competing claims into propositions about our own attitudes and behavioral dispositions towards the world. Once cast in pragmatic terms, we shall find that either the competing claims mean the same thing (i.e., they result in attitudes leading to the same kind of action), or that one frustrates while the other assists action. James argues that as this is, for better or worse, a world which demands that we *act*, we should adopt those metaphysical propositions which facilitate action, support our efforts, and underwrite our deepest hopes.

The Pragmatic Conception of Truth

We have been dealing with James's account of how pragmatism addresses disputes in metaphysics. We may say that a dispute is metaphysical when observational evidence is insufficient to determine the question either way. So, returning to the above example, the dispute between materialism and spiritualism cannot be settled by simply *looking* at the world. Science can tell us about how material bodies behave and interact, but science cannot tell us whether everything that exists is material. Of course, not all disputes are like this. Furthermore, it does not follow that James is advocating a view according to which I should believe that I have a million dollars in my pocket if this belief will lift my spirits and hence facilitate action. Such a view would be silly. In the case of the million dollars in my pocket, observational evidence *is* sufficient to settle the question. I examine the contents of my pocket and discover that it *is not true* that I have a million dollars there.

What does follow for James is, however, that pragmatism is not only a method of dealing with metaphysics, it is also "a certain theory of truth" (WWJ, 381). James's "Pragmatic Conception of Truth" is perhaps the most controversial product of philosophy in the twentieth century; it was the subject of extreme debate in the years following publication of *Pragmatism*, and it remains central to contemporary discussions of truth. To this theory we now turn.

To begin, suppose someone says, "Lincoln was assassinated." Clearly, this statement is true. But what do we mean by calling it true? Many philosophers have promoted what is known as the *correspondence theory of truth*. On this view, a statement is true if it "agrees with" or "corresponds to" the way the world is or "reality." So, on this view, the

47

statement "Lincoln was assassinated" is true because Lincoln was assassinated; accordingly the statement "Nixon was assassinated" is false because Nixon died of natural causes. Of course, this is simply common sense. A decidedly philosophical issue does emerge, however, once it is asked *how it is possible* that a statement—a bit of language—can bear a *relation* such as agreement or correspondence to a non-linguistic *state of affairs*. How can a sentence *P*, denote a situation *X*? In what does the relation of "correspondence to reality" consist?

Philosophers have puzzled over this question for centuries with little success. James weighs in with the pragmatic theory of truth as an attempt to apply the pragmatic method in analyzing the notions of agreement and correspondence. James writes:

> Pragmatism...asks its usual question. "Grant an idea or belief to be true," it says, "what concrete difference will its being true make in anyone's actual life? How will the truth be realized? What experiences will be different from those which would obtain if the belief were false? What, in short, is the truth's cash-value in experiential terms?" (WWJ, 430)

Appropriating Peirce's theory that a belief is essentially a proposal for action, James answers:

> To 'agree' in the widest sense with a reality *can only mean to be guided either straight up to it or into its surroundings, or to be put into such working touch with it as to handle either it or something connected with it better than if we disagreed.*
> (WWJ, 434)

That is, on the Jamesian analysis "[t]he essential thing is the process of being guided" in action; "correspondence to the way the world is" and "agreement with reality" are "essentially...affair[s] of leading" (WWJ, 435):

> Any idea that helps us to *deal* whether practically or intellectually, with either the reality or its belongings, that doesn't entangle our progress in frustrations, that *fits*, in fact, and adapts our life to the reality's whole setting will agree sufficiently to...hold true of that reality. (WWJ, 435)

To say that a given statement is true, then, is to say that, were one to believe it, one would be successfully led in action. A statement is true, then, insofar as it is a reliable guide for action. Insofar as a statement frustrates action, it is false.

One does not need much training in philosophy to anticipate the kinds of objections that have been raised against James's theory of truth. It has seemed to many critics that James is suggesting that those statements which we should *like* to be true are *ipso facto* true. Indeed, many of James's more casual remarks in proposing his theory invite such an interpretation. Consider a few of the most notorious claims:

> The true, to put it very briefly, is only the expedient in our way of thinking.... (WWJ, 438)

> Our account of truth is an account of truths in the plural...having only this quality in common, that they *pay*. (WWJ, 436)

> You can say...that 'it is useful because it is true' or that 'it is true because it is useful'. Both these phrases mean exactly the same thing.... (WWJ, 431)

Given these remarks, it may seem that, according to James, truth consists in simply the usefulness, expediency, or profitableness of a proposition, and this is often how we use the term 'pragmatic' in our everyday language. Were this the view that James is advocating, it would admit of an easy refutation since there are many propositions which may be useful to believe but nonetheless false. Many of James's critics have taken him to be promoting just the kind of simplistic view that the above comments seem to suggest. As A. J. Ayer put it:

> These objections are so obvious that it is hard to understand how James could have remained unmoved by them *if* he *really* held the views against which they were directed.[13]

However, James's view is in fact a great deal more sophisticated than it may first appear, and many of James's most trenchant critics have often underestimated the subtleties of James's position.[14]

A full explication and defense of James's view cannot be undertaken here. We can, however, address some of the principal misconceptions driving the most common criticisms. We think the most prominent criticisms share a common flaw in that they attempt to understand James's conception of truth in isolation from his pragmatism and radical empiricism. That this is a mistake should be evident from the fact that James titles his chapter on truth in *Pragmatism*, "Pragmatism's Conception of

Truth"; James's account of truth is continuous with his more general philosophical approach and must be understood in that context.

Typical objections to James's theory attempt to devise cases in which it is useful or expedient to believe something that's plainly false. Of particular importance to understanding properly James's theory of truth, however, is the radically empirical conception of experience it presupposes. With this in mind, let us consider the case of a beggar who finds it useful to believe that he has a million dollars in his pocket.[15] Surely James, of all philosophers, is the first to place value on the psychological consequences of belief. And yet, what is James to say about the common sense consideration that, no matter how useful it is to the beggar to believe himself wealthy, it is nonetheless *false* that he has a million dollars. Clearly, this seems to be a decisive refutation of James's theory. However, the proposed refutation misconstrues the sense of James's appeal to the "useful." Of course, the beggar may find comfort in the belief that he is wealthy, and to this small extent, we can say the belief is "useful" and that the belief "pays," yet when we note that, for James, experience is not a collection of distinct sensory events, but a continuous flow of life, we see that the usefulness of the beggar's momentary relief is at best fleeting and, when placed in the context of the entire stream of experience, not useful at all.

To see this, recall that James retains Peirce's functionalist account of belief: the meaning of a belief is the habit of action it produces, and every meaningful belief thus has a *purpose* insofar as it is adopted for the sake of successful action. But habit and action are not to be understood simply as individual events, isolated *doings*. Just as habits implicate the environment as well as the organism, all action occurs within a complex network of experience. For example, the act of taking a sip of coffee involves the coordination within experience of a wide variety of factors: my beliefs about the location of the coffee and how the cup is to be grasped, the common sense trust in the existence and general stability of medium-sized physical objects, the working against gravity and other physical forces that keep the cup in place, among others. Given that actions occur within the manifold of experience, it is perhaps more correct to think of a belief as a guide for *activity*. Now, the pragmatic conception of truth maintains that beliefs are to be evaluated according to their ability to guide activity; accordingly, beliefs "become true just in so far as the help us to get into satisfactory relation with other parts of our experience" (WWJ, 382). Hence the "usefulness" James associates with the truth of a proposition has to do with its ability to guide action successfully *within* the whole of experience. To repeat, "The essential thing is the process of being guided. Any idea that helps us to *deal*...with either the reality or its belongings... and adapts our life to reality's whole setting, will...hold true of that reality" (WWJ, 435).

In our scenario, for instance, the moment of relief generated by the beggar's belief that he has a million dollars does not comprise the whole of his experience, and so does not constitute the usefulness of the idea. The remaining portion of the beggar's experience will frustrate the belief that he has a million dollars, and any action based on the idea (e.g., trying to buy a new car, attempting to get a home mortgage, and so forth) will entangle him in frustrations. The belief is false, no matter how pleasurable it may be to hold it.

So it is with all our beliefs. Those beliefs are true which successfully direct action, those beliefs are false which do not. Of course, this conception denies that truth is a "stagnant" property that inheres in true propositions (WWJ, 430). As James says, "Truth *happens* to an idea," it "*becomes* true, it is *made* true by events" (WWJ, 430). That is, beliefs are *made* true through the actions they guide. Accordingly, truths are constantly subject to revision in light of new experience; as "experience...has a way of *boiling over*, and making us correct our present formulas," all of our current truths are "temporary" (WWJ, 438). We may imagine an "ideal vanishing point towards which all our temporary truths will some day converge," but "we have to live today by what truth we can get today, and be ready tomorrow to call it falsehood" (WWJ, 438).

The Career of Pragmatism

The two principal components of James's pragmatism have now been discussed, but before moving on to our discussion of the moral implications of James's thought, a few comments about the career of pragmatism are in order.

We noted above that whereas James credits Peirce with originating both the term 'pragmatism' and the pragmatic maxim, we have seen that he charges that Peircean pragmatism is too narrow. Peirce saw the pragmatic maxim as a way to dismiss metaphysical disputes as meaningless. James, by contrast, employed the pragmatic method as a way of making the meanings of competing metaphysical claims clear by cashing out the psychological and dispositional implications of adopting them. Hence, for James, metaphysics was not, as Peirce claimed, a collection of "meaningless" and "absurd" (5.423) propositions. We may say that, according to James, Peircean pragmatism is too tough-minded. In a remark that calls Peirce to mind, James writes:

> One misunderstanding of pragmatism is to identify it with positivistic tough-mindedness, to suppose that it scorns every rationalistic notion as so much jabber and gesticulation, that it loves intellectual anarchy as such as prefers a sort of wolf-world absolutely unpent and wild and without a master or a collar to any philosophic classroom product whatsoever. (WWJ, 460)

For his part, Peirce in 1905 recognized that

> It probably has never happened that a philosopher has attempted to give a general name to his own doctrine without that name's soon acquiring in common philosophical usage, a signification much broader than was originally intended. (5.413)

And in this light, Peirce's reaction against James's pragmatism was swift. In a letter shortly following the publication of James's *Pragmatism*, Peirce charged James with planting the "seeds of death" (6.485) into the pragmatist doctrine. He resolved to "kiss his child [viz., pragmatism] good-bye and relinquish it to its higher destiny." Peirce rebaptized his philosophy 'pragmaticism', a name he hoped was "ugly enough to be safe from kidnappers" (5.414). The differences between Peirce and James regarding the nature and scope of pragmatism has lead one commentator ·to remark "perhaps it would be correct, and just to all parties, to say that the modern movement known as pragmatism is largely the result of James's having misunderstood Peirce"; this certainly would have satisfied Peirce.[16]

It is clear, then, that 'pragmatism' may not be a term that denotes a universally accepted meaning,[17] and Peirce was not the only early proponent of pragmatism who sought to distance himself from James's ideas. Along with Peirce and James, John Dewey (1859-1952) rounds out the trio typically identified as the "classical" pragmatists.[18] At the time James's *Pragmatism* appeared, Dewey was teaching at the Columbia University having gained considerable notoriety as head of the Laboratory School and department of philosophy at the University of Chicago, and had written influential works such as "The Reflex Arc Concept in Psychology" (1896), that was itself greatly influenced by James's *Principles of Psychology*. In recognition of Dewey as head of the "Chicago school" of pragmatism, James even makes reference to Dewey throughout his *Pragmatism*. In his own 1908 review of *Pragmatism*, "What Pragmatism Means by 'Practical'," however, Dewey writes,

> Since Mr. James has referred to me as saying "truth is what gives satisfaction," I may remark (apart from the fact that I do not think I ever said that truth is what *gives* satisfaction) that I have never identified any satisfaction with the truth of an idea, save *that* satisfaction which arises when the idea as working hypothesis or tentative method is applied to prior existences in such a way as to fulfill what it intends.[19]

Shortly after this philosophical controversy concerning James's *Pragmatism*, Dewey dropped the term 'pragmatism' as a characterization of his philosophical approach, preferring terms like "experimentalism," "naturalism," and "instrumentalism."[20]

* * *

Though interest in pragmatist thought dropped dramatically in the 1960s as new styles of philosophizing came to prominence, since its inception at the turn of the last century, pragmatism has been an influential philosophical perspective. And while many contemporary philosophers, such as John Lachs, John J. McDermott, Beth Singer and others, continue to work within classical pragmatist scholarship, since the 1980s, there has been a "neo-pragmatism" movement steadily growing among philosophers in America. Contemporary figures in philosophy such as Richard Rorty, Hilary Putnam, Susan Haack, and Cornel West have put the insights of the original pragmatists to work within the contexts of current philosophical debate.[21] Not unlike that of their philosophical forefathers, the work of the neo-pragmatists has met with thorough, and sometimes harsh, criticism.[22] Nonetheless, there is no denying that pragmatist ideas are once again the center of philosophical discussion and debate.

Endnotes

[1] See Cornelis de Wal's *On Peirce* (Belmont, CA: Wadsworth, 2001) for a full and accessible examination of Peirce's thought.

[2] The account of the origin of pragmatism that follows is drawn from remarks by Peirce in a 1906 manuscript (5.11-5.13). It is also worth

noting that Peirce offers a genealogy of the term "pragmatism" that differs from James's; see 5.412.

[3] Originally published in *Popular Science Monthly* in the years 1877 and 1878, respectively, as the first two installments in a series of six papers collectively entitled *Illustrations of the Logic of Science.* Interestingly, neither of these essays contains the word 'pragmatism'. For Peirce's explanation, see 5.13.

[4] Cf. citation in Chapter 1, n11.

[5] Cf. 5.373 and 5.397.

[6] The example is Peirce's, cf. 5.403.

[7] We will see in Chapter 3 a decided difference between Peirce and James on just this debate.

[8] Hegel, *Philosophy of Right*, Knox, trans. (Oxford University Press, 1952), 10. For James's most mocking assessment of Hegel, see "On Some Hegelisms" (WTB, 263-298).

[9] Cf. Hegel's *Phenomenology of* Spirit, Miller, trans. (New York: Oxford University Press, 1977), and for a discussion of Hegelian philosophy see Allison Leigh Brown, *On Hegel* (Belmont, CA: Wadsworth, 2001).

[10] Cf. citation in Chapter 1, n12.

[11] Hume 1978, 269. See Chapter 1, n12 for full citation.

[12] James's' student, George Santayana, comes to a similar conclusion about any skeptical approach to philosophy in his work *Scepticism and Animal Faith* (New York: C. Scribners), 1923.

[13] A. J. Ayer, *The Origins of Pragmatism*, (San Francisco: Freeman, Cooper and Co.), 1968, 198 (emphsis added).

[14] The classic criticisms are found in Bertrand Russell's "William James's Conception of Truth" (in Russell's *Philosophical Essays* [London: Allen and Unwin, 1966], 112-130) and G. E. Moore's "Professor James's 'Pragmatism'" (*Proceedings of the Aristotelian Society* 8 [1907]: 33-77). James published a collection of his papers defending his theory of truth in 1909 titled *The Meaning of Truth* (Cambridge: Harvard University Press, 1975). D. C. Phillips' "Was William James Telling the Truth After All?" (*The Monist* 68 [1984]: 419-34), Moreland Perkins' "Notes on the Pragmatic Theory of Truth" (*The Journal of Philosophy* 49 [1952]: 573-87), and Hilary Putnam's "James's Theory of Truth" (in Ruth A. Putnam, ed. *The Cambridge Companion to William James*. New York: Cambridge University Press, 1997) all pro-

vide nice surveys of the philosophical issues. The Russell, Moore, Phillips and Perkins essays are available along with other commentaries and James's Pragmatism lectures in Doris Olin, ed., *William James–Pragmatism in Focus*, (London: Routledge, 1992).

[15] We recognize that this example is not a richly complicated (unlike, for instance, the problem of false beliefs about one's own personality may be), but we believe it is better to understand James's theory through easier examples before attempting more difficult applications. We refer the reader to the "Selected Readings" at the end of the book for discussions of the deeper complexities.

[16] Perry 1996, 281. (Full citation available at the end of the book in "Selections for Further Reading.")

[17] As early as 1908, A. O. Lovejoy argued, disparagingly, that the meanings of 'pragmatism' were multiple and irreducible. See his "The Thirteen Pragmatisms" *Journal of Philosophy*, v. 5, 5-12, 29-39.

[18] Other figures among the classical pragmatist tradition include many of the colleagues of Dewey's during his time at the University of Chicago (1894-1904), including G. H. Mead, J. R. Angell, A. Moore, and others.

[19] In Hester and Talisse, eds., *Essays in Experimental Logic* (Carbondale: Southern Illinois University Press, 2003).

[20] See Talisse, *On Dewey* (Belmont, CA: Wadsworth, 2000) for a full account of Dewey's philosophy.

[21] See Rorty's *Philosophy and the Mirror of Nature* (Princeton, NJ: Princeton University Press, 1979). Also see Putnam's *Pragmatism: An Open Question* (Cambridge: Blackwell, 1995), Haack's *Evidence and Inquiry* (Cambridge: Blackwell, 1993), and West's *The American Evasion of Philosophy* (Madison: University of Wisconsin Press, 1989).

[22] For the current debates in general, see Morris Dickstein (ed.), *The Revival of Pragmatism* (Durham, NC: Duke University Press, 1998). For debates specific to Rorty, see Saatkamp, ed. *Rorty and Pragmatism* (Nashville: Vanderbilt University Press, 1995).

4

Pluralism and the Moral Life

Will not every one instantly declare a world fitted only for
fair-weather human beings susceptible of every passive en-
joyment, but without independence, courage, or fortitude, to
be from a moral point of view incommensurably inferior to a
world framed to elicit from the man every form of triumphant
endurance and conquering moral energy?

—"The Sentiment of Rationality" (WWJ, 340)

Moral Experience

We have emphasized throughout this study James's radically empirical approach to philosophy. Recall once again that the radical empiricist
is committed to experience in all its wild intensity and irreducible variety.
Accordingly James rejects traditional empiricism for holding what he
sees as an unduly tidy view of experience; according to traditional empiricism, experience comes in discrete packets of "sensation" (WWJ, 292-
293). He likewise rejects rationalism for its abandonment of experience
in favor of an equally tidy and secure universe that forms a rational whole,
what James calls a "block universe" (WWJ, 595). James contends that
both views commit the same error insofar as they turn away from the va-
garies of lived experience for the sake of theorizing a world that is finished, complete, and tame. Yet experience teaches that our world is *not* a
finished, rational whole and *not* reducible to the scientists' atoms and
laws; we live, instead, in a "half-wild, half-saved universe" (WTB, 61) in

which "possibilities, not finished facts, are the realities with which we have actively to deal" (WTB, 62).

We have seen that James's commitment to lived experience brings with it a series of philosophical implications. In preceding chapters, we saw how radical empiricism leads James to adopt a certain metaphysics, a certain theory of meaning, a certain conception of truth, and a certain philosophical methodology. Hence the discussion thus far has been mostly academic; we have placed James in the wider context of traditional Philosophy. Yet, as was argued in the introductory chapter, James must not be read as solely an academic philosopher. The principal objective of a radically empirical philosophy is to "return to life"; that is, to bring philosophical ideas and habits consciously to bear on our lives.

Among the irreducible components of our lived experience is what we shall call "moral experience." That is, our daily transactions with others and the world feature a decidedly *moral* dimension. Just as the world *forces* us to hold beliefs and thus to act, we are likewise compelled to make judgments about good and evil, responsibility and forgiveness, beauty and ugliness, virtue and vice. According to the radical empiricist, these judgments, and the elements of experience that compel them, are as real as any other aspect of experience. Hence your visual experience of the ink spots on this page which comprise this very sentence is, on the view of the radical empiricist, on a par with your judgment that your favorite painting is a work of beauty, your feeling of regret at the remembrance of a missed opportunity to do good, and your repulsion to the idea of the unnecessary suffering of innocents. Unlike traditional philosophical systems, which attempt either to reduce moral experience to something more scientifically manageable such as pleasure and pain, or to elevate moral experience to something other-worldly, supernatural, and as such inexplicable, the radical empiricist bids us to confront the facts of experience directly and on their own terms. This follows from the basic tenets of radical empiricism.

Regarding moral experience, it is our view that James's examination of the implications of a radically empirical approach to what he calls the "moral life" marks the culmination of his thought, the moment towards which all else points. In this chapter, we shall develop James's moral vision by means of a series of encounters with topics such as determinism, pluralism, risk, and religious belief. These might at first seem a collection of disparate and unassociated themes, but, according to James, from the radically empirical point of view they are essential topics in the analysis of the moral life. Our own analysis of James's thought requires that we discuss these factors singularly, but successful analysis on our part should in the end demonstrate successful synthesis of them as well.

Determinism, Possibility, and Pluralism

The Problem of Free Will

A long standing concern in philosophy, the problem of free will traditionally consists in reconciling our prevailing self-image as free agents capable of choosing our own actions through the force of our own will alone with a scientific world-view according to which *all* present events, including human actions, are the law-abiding outcomes of previous events. Put another way, science tells us that events at the level of everyday experience are *determined* by prior events. In fact, the very *success* of science confirms this—scientists are able to make predictions precisely because future events follow from present events in law-like ways. So, for example, were I to drop a cube of sodium into a vat of water, there would be an explosion. I know this because chemists have established that sodium and water interact so as to bring about an explosion. In fact, given sufficient information about the volume of water, the amount of sodium, and other environmental conditions, a chemist can predict precisely the *kind* of explosion one may expect. Given the laws that govern the physical events in our universe, whenever sodium is introduced into a vat of water, there *necessarily* will be an explosion unless some other factor interferes so as to *inhibit* the reaction. But of course, the presence of the inhibitor makes it *necessary* that no explosion should occur. The point is simple: when there is an explosion, it is the *necessary* outcome of prior events. Alternately, we can see this point from the other side of the coin; it would be silly to say that the explosion was a *random* matter, that where the mixing of sodium and water produced an explosion there *might not have been* that explosion. These law-like regularities are both the stuff and the prerequisite of physical science, whose general mission it is to discover the laws which govern physical events so that certain events might be avoided and others brought into being.

We need not turn to the chemistry lab, however, for examples of how present events are determined by prior events. We adopt this attitude whenever we seek an *explanation* for some unanticipated occurrence. Imagine the following scenario: You get into your car, turn the ignition, and, contrary to your expectation, the car does not start. What would you conclude? Certainly, you would instantly believe that there was *something wrong* with the machinery of the car—a broken ignition switch, an empty gas tank, a dead battery, or some such condition. You expect that some prior event, such as the battery going dead, is the *cause* of the car's inability to start; without a properly functioning battery, the car *cannot* start. The important point here is that you *expect* to find some *cause* of the car's failure to start, some defect or malfunction making it *necessary* that the car would not start. If you cannot find the cause yourself, and want the car to start, you will get the car to a mechanic with instructions to find the problem and correct it.

Now imagine what your reaction would be to a mechanic who, after examining your car, concluded that there was *nothing* wrong with it; not that he could *find* nothing wrong, but that, in fact, *nothing was wrong*. *Finding* nothing wrong means that the mechanic cannot *locate* the cause of the car's failure to start; he admits the *existence* of the cause of the car's failure, but asserts that he cannot find it. By contrast, though, to say that there is *nothing* wrong with the car is to say that there is *no cause* for the car's failure to start, that the car's failure is entirely unrelated to its mechanical condition. However, in the face of a car that will not start, if your mechanic claimed that there was no cause for your car's failure, you would with good reason look for a new mechanic. Such is the force in our thinking of the view that present events are causally determined by prior events *with necessity*.

These examples might strike you as commonplace and not particularly engaging on the philosophical level. In part, this is because we are confident that human behavior is substantively different from the behavior of cars and sodium. This might be true, but it is difficult to explain exactly in what this important difference consists. To see this, consider that when one wants to explain another person's behavior, one typically appeals to things like the person's desires, beliefs, and purposes. But is there some great difference between saying "Mary walked into the hall because she wanted a drink from the water fountain" and "The car would not start because the battery was dead"? Would it not be just as odd to say that Mary walked into the hall *for no reason* as it would to say that the car failed to start for no reason? In both cases we rightfully *expect* there to be a cause for the observed behavior. Of course, the causes of the car's failure to start are often more easily discerned than the causes of human behavior; yet recall the distinction drawn above between being able to *find* a cause and there being one. It does not follow that since we are

59

much better at finding causes when it comes to cars and explosions, prior events do not out of necessity cause human actions.

James's Analysis of Determinism

Determinism, then, is the view according to which every event is the necessary outcome of the causal force of prior events. If determinism is true, then every event is *necessary*. Put another way, nothing that has happened could have failed to happen, and nothing that has failed to happen could have happened. The determinist asserts that for any event that has occurred, that event *must have been*, and it was strictly *impossible* for any other event to have occurred in its place. In James's words, determinism says that "those parts of the universe already laid down absolutely appoint and decree what the other parts shall be," and that "the future has no ambiguous possibilities hidden in its womb" (WWJ, 590). From this, we can infer that the thesis known as *indeterminism* maintains that "the parts have a certain amount of play on one another, so that the laying down of one of them does not necessarily determine what the others shall be" (WWJ, 591). Hence, according to the indeterminist, there is a plurality of distinct possible futures, each of which is entirely consistent with the causal tendencies of this very moment and its past. In short, determinism denies that there are real *possibilities* whereas indeterminism embraces possibility and rejects the idea that everything is necessary (WWJ, 591).

So far our discussion of the determinist and indeterminist theses has been overtly philosophical, but in keeping with his pragmatism, James contends that the debate taken as a strictly philosophical question is insoluble (WWJ, 596) or, recalling our discussion of the pragmatic method, interminable. To demonstrate this we shall draw upon a modified version of James's own example developed in his 1884 essay, "The Dilemma of Determinism" (WWJ, 593f.). Let us allow for the sake of argument the indeterminist's view that possibilities are real, and consider that at this very moment some person, call her Alice, is confronted with two options. On the one hand, Alice may continue reading this sentence; on the other, she may stop reading and attend to something else. We may hence speak of there being two alternate possible universes: one in which Alice continues reading, and one in which she stops reading. Of course, only one of these possible universes can be the *actual* universe: *either* Alice will continue, *or* she will stop—she cannot do both. Now let us imagine ourselves in a position from which we may view the realization of both pos-

Pluralism and the Moral Life

sibilities; that is, we first imagine that the universe in which Alice continues is actualized, and then we imagine that the universe in which she stops reading is instead actualized.

On the determinist's view, exactly one of these universes is strictly *impossible* and the other is strictly *necessary*. In other words, the determinist maintains that *exactly one* of these universes is consistent with the causal force of prior events, and that the other universe is strictly *inconsistent* with the causal history of the universe. Here James asks of the determinist, "looking out at these universes, can you say which is the impossible and accidental one, and which is the rational and necessary one?" (WWJ, 594). How is the universe in which Alice continues reading to be distinguished from the world in which she stops? Recalling the pragmatic dictum that there is no difference that does not *make* a difference (WWJ, 397), James asks determinists to specify to what the difference between the necessary and the impossible comes.

Let us suppose that Alice in fact continued reading at the moment we hypothesized. James argues that the determinist can assert only *after the fact* that the event of Alice's continuing to read was necessary from the point of view of the universe's entire past. Yet James insists that *prior* to the fact of Alice's continued reading, the determinist cannot point to any feature of her stopping that would render it an impossibility. That is, prior to the fact of Alice's continuing to read, both her continuing and her stopping seem to the determinist equally possible outcomes. Hence, there is no discernable difference between an *impossibility* and a *necessity*, between the event which *must be* and the event which *cannot be*. We may ask, then, what kind of necessity is this that cannot be distinguished from impossibility? How can the determinist's conception of *necessity* in practice be distinguished from her conception of *impossibility*? Her position founders on the pragmatic maxim.

Regret

James does not put the issue to rest here. It is important for him to emphasize the practical implications of accepting determinism. Chief among these implications is the status of moral experience. In particular, it is difficult to make sense of ordinary moral language and judgment if we accept that every event occurs necessarily. To demonstrate this, James appeals to a news story involving the confession of a murderer. He writes,

> Hardly any one can remain *entirely* optimistic after reading
> the confession of the murderer at Brockton the other day:
> how, to get rid of his wife, whose continued existence bored
> him, he inveighed her into a desert spot, shot her four times,
> and then, as she lay on the ground and said to him "You didn't
> do it on purpose, did you, dear?" replied, "No, I didn't do it on
> purpose," as he raised a rock and smashed her skull. (WWJ,
> 597)

The example is deliberately chosen to evoke a strong moral reaction. In particular, when we read of such events, we feel a sense of frustration, outrage, and/or pathos; in sum, we feel *regret*. We judge that the murder depicted above *should not* have happened, and we lament that it has. This phenomenon of regret is pervasive in our experience; as James notes, "Hardly an hour passes in which we do not wish that something might be otherwise" (WWJ, 596).

And yet, what will the determinist say of the Brockton murder? Since on the determinist's view every event is the necessary outcome of prior events, he must say "the murder...[was] necessary from eternity...nothing else for a moment had a ghost of a chance of being put into [its] place" (WWJ 597). But to this, James replies,

> If this Brockton murder was called for by the rest of the uni-
> verse, if it had to come at its preappointed hour, and if nothing
> else would have been consistent with the sense of the whole,
> what are we to think of the universe? (WWJ, 597)

In such a universe as countenanced by the determinist, our judgment of regret at the murder is nonsense, since it entails that the impossible should be. James explains,

> The judgment of regret calls murder bad. Calling a murder
> bad means, if it mean anything at all, that the thing ought not
> to be, that something else ought to be in its stead. Determin-
> ism, in denying that anything else can be in its stead, virtually
> defines the universe as a place in which what ought to be is
> impossible,—in other words, as an organism whose constitu-
> tion is affected with an incurable taint, and irremediable flaw.
> (WWJ, 597)

Hence, the determinist position dooms us to a passive acceptance of "what is," ruling out, in James's terms, what "ought to be," for it rules out the efficacy of human action. In this way, the determinist thesis runs

Pluralism and the Moral Life

counter to the fundamental commitments of radical empiricism insofar as it both denies such efficacy and rejects an important aspect of moral experience. Determinism denies the efficacy of human action in that it denies that human will can bring about anything whose existence is not already causally necessary, and it rejects moral experience insofar as it makes a shambles of our ordinary moral judgments, such as the judgment that the Brockton murder is regrettable. Yet, according to James, we are *compelled* to make moral judgments, and we cannot understand ourselves and our actions except in *in*determinist terms. James writes,

> I cannot understand the willingness to act, no matter how we feel, without the belief that acts are really good and bad. I cannot understand the belief that an act is bad, without regret as its happening. I cannot understand regret without the admission of real, genuine possibilities in the world. Only *then* is it other than a mockery to feel, after we have failed to do our best, that an irreparable opportunity is gone from the universe, the loss of which it must forever mourn. (WWJ, 605)

Accordingly, the first implication of radical empiricism for our moral experience is that we must reject determinism and the pessimism that it engenders. Rejecting determinism does not mean that we must embrace a chaotic or random world; rather the rejection of determinism entails the commitment to the reality of *possibilities* whose actualization depends in part upon how we act. Accordingly, the indeterminist sees the universe not as a "solid block" (WWJ, 595) of "unbending" fact (WWJ, 591), but instead as open and pluralistic, as "vulnerable, and liable to be injured by certain of its parts if they act wrong" (WWJ, 606). Wrong action is thus seen as a "matter of possibility or accident, neither inevitable nor yet to be infallibly warded off" (WWJ, 606). Hence the pluralistic universe of the indeterminist is not a world that is necessarily *good*, but a world that holds the *possibility* of good. In James's words, indeterminism means simply the "chance that in moral respects the future may be other and better than the past has been" (WWJ, 607). It is important to emphasize that James's indeterminism offers no guarantee that the universe *will* improve; James does not replace the pessimism of determinism with the naïve optimism typical of rationalist philosophies. As we have mentioned before and will discuss in more detail below, James's position is a "meliorism" where moral experience requires that we accept pluralism, and pluralism simply means that it is *possible* that one may through her action improve the world.

The Moral Life

Morality in an Open Universe

Thus far we have been discussing pluralism as primarily a *metaphysical* thesis, a thesis about the innermost nature of reality. Specifically, we have said that pluralism is the thesis that maintains that possibility is a real feature of the universe, that the past does not *entirely* fix the future. We have seen that this openness accounts for the potency of human will and the meaningfulness of our moral experiences. Yet this is only one aspect of the pluralist thesis. The openness of the universe and the reality of possibility also entail the unsettling result that uncertainty and risk are real, that insecurity and danger are inextricable elements of our world. That is, on the pluralist view that James advocates, our understanding of ourselves and our ability to control our universe is necessarily limited; every intellectual picture of the world must be incomplete, "Truth's fullness is elusive; ever not quite, not quite!" (WWJ, 347). However, these limitations are not merely due to the incompleteness of *our* intellectual capacities; knowledge is limited, understanding incomplete, and truth elusive because *the universe itself* does not constitute a finished, final fact; a pluralistic universe is dynamic and open, resisting final analyses and ultimate formulations. Accordingly "none of our explanations are complete" (WWJ, 320).

Hence pluralism has important implications for morality. According to James pluralism implies that "neither the whole of truth nor the whole of good is revealed to any single observer"; thus, "No one has insight into all the ideals" (WWJ, 645). Of course, this is a fairly abstract formulation. To get a better sense of the moral implications of pluralism, consider James's account of an episode in his own experience:

> Some years ago, while journeying in the mountains of North Carolina, I passed by a large number of 'coves', as they call them there, or heads of small valleys between the hills, which had been newly cleaned and planted. The impression on my mind was one of unmitigated squalor. The settler had in every case cut down the more manageable trees, and left their charred stumps standing. The larger trees he had girdled and

killed, in order that their foliage should not cast a shade. He had then built a log cabin, plastering its chinks with clay, and had set up a tall zigzag raid fence around the scene of his havoc, to keep the pigs and cattle out. Finally, he had irregularly planted the intervals between the stumps and trees with Indian corn, which grew among the chips; and there he dwelt with his wife and babes—an axe, a gun, a few utensils, and some pigs and chickens feeding in the woods being the sum total of his possessions. (WWJ, 630-631)

James uses loaded language to describe the scene, and his initial estimation is unqualifiedly negative:

> The forest had been destroyed; and what had 'improved' it out of existence was hideous, a sort of ulcer, without a single element of artificial grace to make up for the loss of Nature's beauty. Ugly, indeed, seemed the life of the squatter...
> (WWJ, 631)

However, upon talking to one of the inhabitants of these coves, James comes to see that he "had been losing the whole inward significance of the situation" (WWJ, 613). He explains,

> Because to me the clearings spoke of naught but denudation, I thought that to those whose sturdy arms and obedient axes had made them they could tell no other story. But, when *they* looked on the hideous stumps, what they thought of was personal victory. The chips, the girdled trees, and the vile spit rails spoke of honest sweat, persistent toil and final reward....
> In short, the clearing, which to me was a mere ugly picture on the retina, was to them a symbol redolent with moral memories and sang a very paean of duty, struggle, and success.... I had been as blind to the peculiar ideality of their condition as they certainly would also have been to the ideality of mine, had they had a peep at my strange academic ways of life at Cambridge. (WWJ, 631)

According to James, this kind of experience "befalls each one of us daily" (WWJ, 630). Most often, we are so wrapped up in our own projects and endeavors that we come to see the world strictly in terms of our own purposes and values. This is, in a sense, unavoidable, "each is bound to feel intensely the importance of his own duties and the significance of the situations that call these forth" (WWJ, 629); yet it is precisely this intensity which leads us to "miss the root of the matter" (WWJ, 630) when it comes to understanding the lives of others. James explains,

> Yet we are but finite, and each one of us has some single specialized vocation of his own. And it seems as if energy in the service of its particular duties might be got only by hardening the heart towards everything unlike them. Our deadness toward all but one particular kind of joy would thus be the price we inevitably have to pay for being practical creatures. (WWJ, 634)

In moral matters, then, each of us suffers from what James calls a "certain blindness" (WWJ, 629) where we (dangerously) judge "other persons' conditions and ideals" (WWJ, 630). And yet, there are occasions, such as the one James describes above, when we overcome this blindness by coming to see matters not simply from our own point of view, but from that of another. On such occasions, we become aware that our feelings and judgments are tied to our own peculiar stations in life; we come to see "how soaked and shot-through life is with values and meanings which we fail to realize because of our external and insensible point of view" (WWJ, 645). Consequently, we come to see that others may be justified in their own feelings and judgments, even when these contradict our own.

The overcoming of moral blindness entails the realization that there is "an exuberant mass of goods" (WWJ, 622) and that these goods do not fit together neatly into a single system of value. As James puts it, "There is hardly a good which we can imagine except as competing for the possession of the same bit of space and time with some other imagined good" (WWJ, 622). There are real contests and real conflicts between different goods—that is, goods are conflicting and, thus, are irreducibly *plural*. In other words, to overcome moral blindness is to embrace *moral pluralism* and, thus, to recognize that the spectrum of goods is so wide and varied that each individual is privy to only a *part* of the good. Each of us is bound to his own particular sense of the good; hence "The very best of men must not only be insensible, but ludicrously and peculiarly insensible, to many goods" (WWJ, 622).

It is important, though, to distinguish James's pluralism about morality from the view known as *moral subjectivism*, or sometimes simply as *relativism*. Moral subjectivists deny that there are any real goods and evils, claiming that all that is required for an action or event to be good is

Pluralism and the Moral Life

that you *believe* or *judge* that it is good. James denies subjectivism, however, insisting that there are *real* goods and evils, and *judging* or *believing* something good is not sufficient for its actually *being* good. Hence the contention of the pluralist is not that good and evil are merely subjective, but rather that our moral experience is necessarily limited to such a degree that no single individual can grasp the *entirety* of good, and no single life can manifest every constituent of the good life. Put another way, the pluralist maintains that there is an irreducible variety of mutually exclusive goods, where "irreducible" means that no single conception of the good can be comprehensive and final, and "mutually exclusive" entails that the realization of one good necessarily precludes the realization of some others. Hence, on James's view, the idea of a morally perfect life is contradictory; no life could realize all the moral goods any more than any single photograph of you could capture all of your features. We are thus resigned to a life in which moral conflict and uncertainty are inexorable. We must act for the best, but we cannot achieve moral perfection; "Some part of the ideal must be butchered" (WWJ, 632).

How We Ought to Live

If James's analysis is correct, we humans are caught in a difficult, perhaps terrifying, predicament. We are compelled by experience to make moral judgments and to commit to certain moral ends. Indeed, much of our lives are bound up with the pursuit of some goal or project, and these pursuits make sense to us only because we take our goals and projects to be *worth* pursuing. *Moral commitment is inevitable.* However, we inhabit a pluralistic universe, and hence our moral commitments capture, at best, only *part* of the good. We are thus led to the proposition that our own moral commitments are perhaps only *as good* as the commitments of others, even when their commitments directly oppose our own. This conflicted state of affairs presses most urgently the primary question of moral philosophy, How ought we to live?

There is no shortage of attempts to answer this question within the tradition of Philosophy where philosophers typically have attempted to *reduce* all moral goods to some single, *summum bonum*, or highest good. Once the *summum bonum* is identified, the mission of moral theory has been to discern a way in which it may be maximized or achieved. That is, traditional moral theories endeavor to discover some set of rules, principles, or commands that can serve to regulate action; they have sought *pre-*

67

scriptions for behavior that can guarantee morally right action. However, according to James, this endeavor is bound to fail for several reasons.

In particular, taking moral experience and pluralism seriously requires that the recognition that there can be no *summum bonum*, no final ranking of all goods, and no "highest" good to which all others are subordinate. Consequently, no moral principle or prescription—nor *set* of principles and prescriptions—can be complete and comprehensive. There is no simple recipe for the good life. As James says, "there is no such thing possible as an ethical philosophy dogmatically made up in advance" (WWJ, 610); "ethical treatises may be voluminous and luminous as well, but they can never be *final*" (WWJ, 626). Experience is too complex and the universe is too rich and varied to allow capture by a few philosophical maxims.

James's rejection of the traditional philosophical aspiration for a comprehensive moral theory, however, does not constitute an abandoning of the fundamental question, How ought we to live? In fact, on James's view this question becomes all the more vital *precisely* because we cannot rely upon tidy philosophical theories for quick-fix solutions to moral dilemmas. We must act in the absence of moral certainty; thus, the question of how we ought to live becomes crucial.

So, how does James approach the question of how we ought to live? To answer this, it is important to recognize that James's rejection of traditional moral theory is in essence a refusal to see the fundamental concern of moral philosophy as focused primarily upon individual *acts*. (Note that we did not pose the question, How ought we to *act*?) The principal focus of Jamesian moral philosophy is *life*, not merely individual actions, and actions are on James's view the expressions or manifestations of our habits, and our habits are formed from our more general *attitude* towards life, not towards specific events. This attitude is what James sometimes refers to as our "mood" (WWJ, 627).

How, then, ought we to live? James's answer is both commonsensical and subtle. Most generally, James advises that we develop what he calls the "strenuous mood," keeping open the stream of moral experience, subjecting oneself to increasingly wider and varied experiences, avoiding the mediocre and the conventional, and resisting the tendency to mechanize or make routine our moral experience. These injunctions may be summarized by saying that the moral life is the life of constantly confronting the question of how we ought to live; James bids us to keep moral questions *open*. This perpetual confrontation forces us always to be ready to reevaluate, revise, and indeed *remake* our lives. Furthermore, we must treat others with respect and tolerance; we must "indulge those whom we see harmlessly interested and happy in their own ways, however unintelligible these may be to us" (WWJ 645). Since pluralism implies that no one has insight into all the ideals, "the first thing to learn in intercourse with others is non-interference with their own peculiar ways of being happy, provided those ways do not assume to interfere by violence with ours" (WWJ, 645).

Meliorism

The Strenuous Mood

The Jamesian moral philosopher is literally concerned with the *moral life*, with the habits and attitudes that tend to promote increasing sensitivity to the human moral predicament. Note, however, that James's call for openness and tolerance is not a call to moral quietism and passivity. Though encouragement of "respect," "tolerance," and "non-interference" lends itself to such a reading, too often the pluralist attitude is mistaken for a stance of "live and let live" which in turn manifests in a moral indifference, a relaxing of moral concerns, what James calls the "easy-going mood" (WWJ, 627). Paradoxically, when the attitude of "live and let live" generates the easy-going mood, the result is a kind of retreat from life. As you may expect, James will have none of this. As we have repeatedly claimed, the whole point of James's philosophy is to facilitate a *return* to life, a heightened mode of *engagement* with the world around us and each other.

The moral life, then, is according to James an *active* life, a life of "sweat and effort" and "struggle," life *in extremis* (WWJ, 648). To see this, consider that pluralism in its most fundamental form entails that ours is an open universe, a universe whose future is yet undetermined, a universe that is still in the making. As we have already noted, an open universe is also a universe of risk and uncertainty, a universe that offers no assurance that good will triumph over evil. Despite this uncertainty, humans are active beings; we are compelled to act on the basis of incomplete information, partial explanations, fallible hypotheses, and, in some instances, wild guesses. The combination of these two aspects of pluralism results in the following: Our actions help create the universe and determine what our lives will become, yet there can be no guarantee in advance of acting that our act will morally improve our situation. Human life is thus a life of continually confronting moral hazards; we must make our way in the world without the benefit of moral certitude. We must act, yet every action carries with it a degree of moral risk; at every turn we have the opportunity to improve the world by means of our actions, yet we always must act under conditions of moral uncertainty. As the universe is itself pluralistic, it is in its very nature neither morally saved nor doomed. Hence human agency is all the more essential, and the question of the moral life all the more urgent—it is *we* who shall make the difference in the "everlasting battle of the powers of light with those of darkness" (WWJ, 639).

As we noted earlier, James calls this the "meliorist" attitude, and in this context, meliorism is the view that stands between moral pessimism and moral optimism (WWJ, 466). The pessimist holds that the world is morally doomed, that evil and depravity are destined to prevail, that any good that the universe may manifest is at best transient and temporary. Conversely, the optimist contends that the universe is destined to be morally saved, that in the end good necessarily will triumph over evil. For James both views constitute a retreat from life. In contrast, pluralists must take the meliorist stance towards the world by rejecting the idea that the moral fate of the universe is laid down in advance of our active contributions to it. Of course, while the meliorist must admit that the universe *may* end with a final victory of evil over good, he merely contends that this victory is not *inevitable*; similarly, the meliorist rejects the idea that the world is inevitably saved. The question of our ultimate moral fate is "once more a case of *maybe*" (WTB 61).

Note that the meliorist view places the *responsibility* for the moral condition of the world upon each of us. As was said above, it is *we* who make the difference between light and darkness, and this difference is constructed at every moment, with every action we perform. That we shoulder ultimate moral responsibility for the world and yet lack the understanding and certainty that would guarantee our moral success makes for a troubling, potentially paralyzing, conundrum. It is easy, in light of our predicament, to feel overwhelmed, and consequently to adopt some comforting variety of moral optimism or pessimism. In so doing, we retreat from life and deny the potency of human agency, but we do not relinquish our responsibility. According to James, we must not allow ourselves to be paralyzed by the difficulties of our predicament; we must not abandon the question of how we ought to live by pretending to have discovered its final answer. The moral life requires the "strenuous mood"

(WWJ, 627), the commitment to the task of *trying* to improve the world *in spite of* moral uncertainty and risk. Hence, the moral life is, for James, a life of struggling to bring about "the largest total universe of good which we can see" (WWJ, 626), all the while realizing that any success we achieve can at best be partial, incomplete, and not final.

Is Life Worth Living?

While not strictly pessimistic, it may seem that James has painted a thoroughly bleak picture of human life: We are caught in a fight that we cannot win; we must participate in an ongoing struggle between good and evil, but we have not the resources to secure a decisive victory; we are called to commit to the meliorist project of improving the world, but we have no guarantee that even our very best efforts can succeed. What kind of life is this?

James admits that the strenuous mood cannot be voluntarily adopted; he cannot *convince* you to undertake the meliorist project. Although "[t]he capacity for the strenuous mood probably lies slumbering in every man," it cannot be summoned at will; rather, "it needs the wilder passions to arouse it" (WWJ, 627). In particular, the strenuous mood is aroused by "the big fears, loves, and indignations; or else the deeply penetrating appeal of some one of the higher fidelities, like justice, truth, or freedom" (WWJ, 627). That is, meliorism cannot be adopted on intellectual grounds; there is no *argument* for meliorism. Rather, the moral life can be taken up only when the appropriate passions have been stimulated by experience. James explains:

> What excites and interests the looker-on at life, what the romances and statues celebrate and the grim civic monuments remind us of, is the everlasting battle of the powers of light with those of darkness...what our human emotions seem to require is the sight of the struggle going on.... Sweat and effort, human nature strained to the uttermost and on the rack, yet getting through alive, and then turning its back on its success to pursue another more rare and arduous still—this is the sort of thing the presence of which inspires us. (WWJ, 648).

James contends that it is in these moments of inspired excitement at the world's travails, in the throws of struggle to realize some ideal, that we come to feel the significance of life. He states,

71

On James

> The significance of life...is the offspring of a marriage of two
> different parents, either of whom alone are barren. The ideals
> taken by themselves give no reality, the virtues by themselves
> no novelty. (WWJ, 657)

Meaningful, significant living, then, requires the active pursuit of what we want to come to pass. On James's view, life is worth living precisely because the world presents us with a plurality of ideals worth fighting for, and precisely because we must risk ourselves in these fights. In fact, James says, "It is only by risking our persons from one hour to another that we live at all" (WTB, 59). Hence pluralism, and the melioristic attitude it generates, provides the conditions under which our lives can have significance. To see this, consider the following from James:

> Suppose the world's author put the case to you before crea-
> tion, saying: "I am going to make a world not certain to be
> saved, a world the perfection of which shall be conditional
> merely, the condition being that each several agent does its
> own 'level best'. I offer you the chance of taking part in such
> a world. Its safety, you see, is unwarranted. It is a real adven-
> ture, with real danger, yet it might win through. It is a social
> scheme of co-operative work genuinely to be done. Will you
> join the procession? Will you trust yourself and trust the other
> agents enough to face the risk?" (WWJ, 468)

In his hypothetical, James gives you the choice: take our world as it is or reject its uncertainty in favor of nothing at all. On James's view, we should accept the offer made to us by this imagined creator because it speaks to our very natures; it is the challenge posed by a pluralistic universe, the *requirement* that we struggle to achieve what we think best, the striving after a moral ideal with no guarantee of success, that makes life meaningful and worth living.

Faith as Courage

We have seen, then, on James's view the moral life consists in the commitment to what we have called the melioristic project. That is, the moral life is one of constant struggle to improve the world. Of course, in light of pluralism, this struggle is multiform—not only do we struggle to realize our moral ideals, we must also struggle to overcome, insofar as possible, the moral blindness to which we are necessarily prone. Put another way, we must strive to realize our ideals, but we must also always be ready to revise those ideals in light of future experience. This willingness to act earnestly in pursuit of a fallible and revisable ideal is what James calls "faith":

> Faith means belief in something concerning which doubt is still theoretically possible; and as the test of belief is willingness to act, one may say that faith is the readiness to act in a cause the prosperous issue of which is not certified in advance. (WWJ, 333)

James, then, identifies "faith" with an attitude concerning action, and particularly with action that has no certitude of producing our desired ends.

However, this may seem like an odd use of the term "faith," for rather than taking faith dispositionally or fortitudinally, most often we talk about faith as a *justification* for believing that some proposition is true. For example, when someone says, "I have faith that God exists," what is typically meant is that faith provides the *basis* for belief; accordingly, one who believes on faith is one who will not be swayed by evidence that runs counter to that belief. James, by contrast, is employing the term, as he says, to characterize the quality of one's commitment to a "cause." To have faith is, on James's view, to be ready to act in pursuit of a cause despite the fact that both the worthiness of the cause and the likelihood of success in attaining it have not been determined in advance. It is in this sense that faith "is in fact that same moral quality which we call courage in practical affairs...." (WWJ, 333). Faith is, according to James, the *courage* to persist in one's moral commitments despite the attendant risks and uncertainties. Again, this faith cannot be voluntarily adopted, and James cannot by means of words and argument persuade you to decide to adopt a melioristic faith; as with courage, faith must be *passional*, it must be *inspired*.

Accordingly, James's use of religious language here is quite deliberate. In fact, James employs religious terms such as "God" to characterize the kind of inspiration that evokes within us the strenuous mood; furthermore, James contends that religious commitment is *necessary* if we are to undertake the meliorist project. James writes, "...in a merely human world without a God, the appeal to our moral energy falls short of its maximal stimulating power" (WWJ, 627); however, "Every sort of energy and endurance of courage and capacity for handling life's evils is set free in those who have religious faith" (WWJ, 628). James concludes, "For this reason, the strenuous type of character will on the battle-field of human history always outwear the easy-going type, and religion will drive irreligion to the wall" (WWJ, 628). Indeed, in keeping with his pragmatic theory of meaning, James maintains that the power of religion to evoke the strenuous mood is in itself sufficient justification for religious belief; James writes,

> The capacity for the strenuous mood lies so deep down among our natural human possibilities that even if there were no metaphysical or traditional grounds for believing in a God, men would postulate one simply as a pretext for living hard, and getting out of the game of existence its keenest possibilities of zest. (WWJ 628)

Of course, like his use of the term 'faith', James's appropriation of the term 'religion' is hardly traditional. "Religion" and "religious experience" are transformed by James's meliorist and radical empiricist turn. Rather than the passive worship of a transcendent entity, "religion" for James is truly *inspirational*, moving us to act for the betterment of ourselves and others precisely when such "betterment" is not guaranteed. "Religious experience" then testifies not to the existence of a transcendent entity *per se*, for "the only thing that [religious experience] testifies to is that we can experience union with *something* larger than ourselves and in that union find our greatest peace" (WWJ, 785). In keeping with the pluralist position, James makes no claims about the necessity of what that "something larger" must be, stating instead that

> the practical needs and experience of religion seem to me sufficiently met by the belief that beyond each man and in a fashion continuous with him there exists a larger power which is friendly to him and to his ideals.... Anything larger will do, if only to be large enough to trust the next step. It need not be infinite, it need not be solitary. It might conceivably even be only a larger and more godlike self, of which the present self would them be but the mutilated expression, and the universe might conceivably be a collection of such selves, of different degrees of inclusiveness, with no absolute unity realized in it at all. (WWJ, 785-786)

Our own discussion in this chapter makes clear that anything that moves us to act towards as-of-yet unrealized ideals can count as the source of religious experience. Further still, however, James's meliorism implies not only that any "something larger" may be a religious source but also requires our commitment and action to bring it to fruition. That is, religion, while serving to *generate* human effort, demands such effort in order to bring about the universe of its belief. Thus, belief, in James's sense, in the face of the unknown and uncertain may be our only way of creating a life worth living, of creating a universe worthy of religious conviction. Such a world and the attitudes that inspire it, which it in turn inspires, require what James calls a *"will* to believe," and it is to this concept and its implications that we turn for our concluding chapter.

5

Religious Commitment to a Moral Universe: James and "The Will to Believe"

When I look at the religious question as it really puts itself to concrete men, and when I think of all the possibilities which both practically and theoretically it involves, then this command that we shall put a stopper on our heart, instincts, and courage and wait...till doomsday, or till such time as our intellect and senses working together may have ranked in evidence enough—this command, I say, seems to me the queerest idol ever manufactured in the philosophic cave.

—"The Will to Believe" (WWJ, 734)

Preliminaries

James's essay, "The Will to Believe," is perhaps his most well-known and controversial essay. In our view, it is also James's single best expression of the themes we have been discussing in this book. We hence conclude our study of James's philosophy with a close examination of this essay. Before turning directly to that examination, however, recall that our discussion in the previous chapter demonstrated how radical empiricism leads to pluralism and eventually to meliorism; in the concluding

76

section of that chapter, we saw how, on James's view, meliorism has a decidedly religious dimension. To repeat, James contends that "religion" is necessary to inspire the strenuous mood; furthermore, the inspirational power of religious belief is sufficient to *justify* religious belief.

The Ethics of Belief

Let us begin with a philosophical question: Can beliefs be justified solely by the positive effects that result from holding those beliefs, or must all beliefs be justified by evidence? To better understand this question, suppose, for example, that I find the proposition that *each of us has an immortal soul that survives bodily death* extremely attractive from the cognitive point of view, and by this I simply mean that the proposition is such that believing it generates a variety of positive *psychological* results: I would experience great comfort knowing that physical death is not the end, my fear of death would relax, my sorrow at the loss of loved ones would be less intense, and so on. Suppose further that these specific psychological results generate a more general sense of happiness and satisfaction with the world; that is, my belief in immortal souls encourages me to be kinder to others, more friendly, and cheerful. Suppose finally that there is *absolutely no evidence that immortal souls exist.* Psychics and so-called mediums once-and-for-all have been discredited, accounts of afterlife experiences all have been shown to be dubious, religious texts are questionable, and the philosophical and theological proofs for immortality are all flawed. Given *these* conditions, would you say that I am *justified* in believing in immortal souls and an afterlife? Importantly, this is *not* to ask whether it is *likely* that I will believe in immortality; it is rather to ask whether I am *warranted* in believing in the absence of evidence.

More generally, we may frame the question: May we believe a proposition when there is no sufficient evidence of its truth? And asking this question engages an area of philosophical inquiry known as the *ethics of belief* wherein it is claimed that each of us has an intellectual *duty* to believe only those propositions that are supported by the best available evidence. On this view, which we shall call *evidentialism*, to believe a proposition on grounds other than evidence is to commit a kind of intellectual sin, or to fail to meet an epistemic obligation. James's younger contemporary, the British philosopher Bertrand Russell (1872-1970), expressed the kernel of evidentialism succinctly when he wrote, "It is undesirable to believe a proposition when there is no ground whatever for supposing it true."[1]

On James

One immediately recognizable implication of evidentialism is that it recommends the *suspension of belief* in cases where the evidence that could decide a certain question is inconclusive. According to the evidentialist, it is better to believe nothing at all than to believe without evidence. On the evidentialist view, when evidence is inconclusive, one should suspend belief until sufficient evidence is secured.

As may already be apparent, the issue of evidentialism is prominent in philosophical discussions of religious belief with evidentialists concluding that religious belief is unwarranted. Returning to our example above, while my psychological states may well be positive and beneficial as a direct result of my belief in immortality, evidentialists maintain that it is wrong for me to believe in immortal souls because the evidence regarding their existence is inconclusive. Note that the evidentialist does not necessarily require that I adopt the belief that there are no immortal souls, for the evidence *against* the existence of souls is likewise inconclusive! On the evidentialist view, it is my intellectual duty to suspend judgment about the existence of souls; the positive psychological effects are simply not sufficient to *justify* my belief. I may elect to inquire further into the matter, but until the evidence decisively favors one or the other proposition, I must believe neither.

A further aspect of evidentialism worth emphasizing is that it aims to make a *categorical* claim about belief. That is, the evidentialist claims that his ethic of belief applies *universally* to all kinds and instances of belief. The striking words of mathematician W. K. Clifford (1845-1879) capture the categorical dimension of evidentialism well. In a frequently quoted passage from his 1877 essay, "The Ethics of Belief," Clifford writes, "It is wrong always, everywhere, and for anyone, to believe anything upon insufficient evidence."[2]

William James's foray into the question of what constitutes a justifiable belief strikes directly at the categorical application of evidentialism. Specifically, in "The Will to Believe," James attacks Clifford's position and, instead, argues in favor of religious belief. It is worth noting that James does *not* argue that the traditional claims of Western religion are decidedly true; in other words, he does not aim to *prove* that, say, God exists or that there are immortal souls. In fact, to undertake such a mission would be to accept the evidentialist ethic of belief, since such an undertaking attempts to show that the evidence in favor of religious belief is decisive. Rather he endeavors to establish two successive claims: First, *in certain cases* evidentialism is in fact *irrational*; second, *religious belief is such a case.*

Again, since James does not attempt to *prove* that some propositions about God and immortality are true, the success of James's argument does not entail that we all ought to adopt some kind of religious belief. James's defense of religious belief, rather, is more a defense of *religious believing.* That is, in "The Will to Believe," James offers "a defense of our right to adopt a believing attitude in religious matters in spite of the fact that our merely logical intellect may not have been coerced" (WWJ, 717). Put otherwise, in this essay, James *concedes* to the evidentialist that the evidence in favor of religious belief is insufficient to "coerce" the intellect into believing, but he maintains that the religious believer is *nonetheless* entitled to her belief and is guilty of no intellectual impropriety in believing.

The argument James deploys in "The Will to Believe" is complex and difficult. Therefore, we do not attempt here to provide a comprehensive analysis of the essay. Many of the more subtle aspects of James's argument will be glossed over, and we shall not attempt to allay some of the problems others have seen in James's argument or respond to some of the more famous objections that have been raised. Moreover, we shall not discuss the fascinating side-issues that James introduces in the essay, of which there are many. We instead hope to make explicit what we take to be the principal line of argument in the essay, to connect this line with the themes previously discussed in this chapter, and to show how this essay serves as a paradigm of Jamesian radical empiricism/meliorism that is at the core of our analysis throughout this book.

Hypotheses and Options

Recall that we said above that James's argument can be understood to progress in two steps where James's first step is to attack evidentialism by showing that there are some cases in which it would be irrational to follow the evidentialists' command to suspend belief in the absence of decisive evidence. However, in order to make his case, James must introduce a system of terms and distinctions regarding beliefs to clarify the debate. So before we can understand fully his attack we must survey these terms and distinctions.

The first term James defines is 'hypothesis', suggesting that we use the term to name "anything that may be proposed to our belief" (WWJ, 717). However, he quickly determines that hypotheses come in two kinds, "live" and "dead," where a live hypothesis "is one which appeals as a real possibility to whom it is proposed" (WWJ, 717) and a dead hypothesis is one which strikes the person to whom it is proposed as so unlikely a candidate for truth that it "refuses to scintillate with any credibility at all" (WWJ, 718). This distinction is not intended to capture any intrinsic property of the hypothesis but concerns rather a subjective estimation of the likelihood of its truth. While you may take many hypotheses to be credible and interesting (if not simply trivial), other hypotheses will strike you as so implausible that they are quite literally *unbelievable*. For example, consider the hypothesis that *the pyramids in Egypt were built by aliens who visited Earth from outer space thousands of years ago.* We confess that we find this hypothesis utterly dead—it strikes us as far beyond the realm of what possibly could be true. We know some people, however, for whom this hypothesis is live at least in the degree to which they are willing to accept it is a *possible* explanation of the existence of the pyramids; and, yes, we even know some for whom the hypothesis is so live that they fully accept it as the explanation of the pyramids.

Liveness (and deadness) of an hypothesis, then, is clearly a matter of degree. But how do we measure the degree of liveness a hypothesis has for us? In good pragmatist fashion, James estimates the degree of liveness of a certain hypothesis for a particular person by reference to that person's willingness to act under the guidance of the hypothesis. "The maximum of liveness in an hypothesis means willingness to act irrevocably" (WWJ, 718), and a maximally live hypothesis is what we call a "belief."

Having defined his use of the term 'hypothesis' and its relationship to "belief," James continues by proposing that we "call the decision between two hypotheses an *option*" (WWJ, 718). And like hypotheses, "options" admit of further analysis. In particular, options may be analyzed according to three categories: An option may be *living* or *dead*; it may be *forced* or *avoidable*; and it may be *momentous* or *trivial*. We shall take each in turn.

Calling upon the prior distinction between kinds of hypotheses, an option is *living* when *both* hypotheses are *live*; otherwise, it is *dead*. Accordingly, the liveness of an option is again a subjective matter. For us, the option, *believe the pyramids were built by aliens, or believe they were built by humans,* is dead because the first hypothesis in the option is, in our view, dead. We might even say that, in this case, no true option has been presented since the first hypothesis is maximally dead for us. On the other hand, the option, *believe that Oswald acted alone in assassinating*

Kennedy, or believe that he was part of a team of assassins, is live for us because "each hypothesis makes some appeal, however small, to [our] belief" (WWJ, 718).

Next, an option is *forced* when the two hypotheses form what logicians call an *exclusive disjunction*, or sometimes a *dilemma*. Consider the option proposed to a thirsty person: *drink beer or drink wine.* This option is not *forced* because it is possible to act in such a way as to satisfy neither hypothesis; one could easily have water, soda, juice, or nothing at all. In other words, the option is *avoidable.* By contrast, consider the option, *drink beer or do not drink beer.* This option is *forced* because it is logically impossible to avoid taking one of the offered choices. Having water, or juice, or nothing at all is logically equivalent to *not drinking beer.* At every moment, you are either drinking beer or you are not drinking beer, thus the option, *drink beer or do not drink beer,* is forced.

Lastly, consider that the forced option, *drink beer or do not drink beer,* is in most instances, a *trivial* option in that your decision is reversible, the offer is repeatable, and, whatever you choose, the decision will not likely drastically affect the rest of your life. By contrast, however, some options are *momentous* insofar as the choice they propose is unique, and once made, irreversible and prone to have consequences for your life in the long run. For a good example of a *momentous* option, consider the position of a person on trial who has something of great significance to gain—such as acquittal—if he commits perjury (and is undetected). The option, *lie under oath, or tell the truth,* is momentous since the choice is unique, irreversible, and at least potentially of great consequence. It is worth noting that the momentousness of an option is, like the liveness and unlike the forcedness, a matter of degree.

From these three "options" categories, James is able to make a further distinction. James calls an option *genuine* whenever such an option proves to be *living, forced,* and *momentous.* A *genuine option* demands our attention and requires some decision, since even avoiding such a decision is itself a choice.

With these categorizations in place, we may now progress to the next step of the argument, which will be to show that the evidentialist ethic of belief is irrational when one is presented with a genuine option that cannot be settled by evidence. In such cases, James contends, we are fully within our epistemic rights to adopt that hypothesis which best satisfies what he calls "our passional nature" (WWJ, 723). That is to say, when confronted with a genuine option that cannot be decided by means of evidence, we may appeal to non-intellectual criteria (such as comfort, desire, and so on) in deciding which hypothesis to adopt.

Against Evidentialism

We begin with James's own statement of his main thesis:

> The thesis I defend is, briefly stated, this: Our *passional* nature not only lawfully may, but must, decide an option between propositions, whenever it is a genuine option that cannot be decided upon intellectual grounds; for to say, under such conditions, "Do not decide, but leave the question open," is itself a passional decision,—just like deciding yes or no,—and is attended with the same risk of losing the truth. (WWJ, 723)

This statement is a bit misleading because it presents as one thesis what are perhaps better understood as two distinct, though closely related, claims. The first is the claim that evidentialism is inapplicable to genuine options that cannot be settled "on intellectual grounds," that is, by appealing to evidence. The second part of James's thesis is a logical point that provides a rationale for the first: When an option is genuine (and hence forced), suspending belief is *equivalent* to adopting one of the hypotheses.

Taking the parts of his thesis in reverse order, let us consider an example roughly based on one James himself offers (WWJ, 730). Suppose a new person has just moved into the vacant residence next door to your home, and you wonder, *Is she a good neighbor, or not?* Further, suppose that this is for you a genuine option: it is "living" insofar as you see both hypotheses as possibly true; it is "forced" insofar as the person will be a good neighbor or not; it is "momentous" insofar as you believe that the goodness or badness of a neighbor can make all the difference between a comfortable living environment and one that is unbearable. Which hypothesis shall you adopt?

Before you answer, however, let us imagine that you have been convinced by Clifford that "it is wrong always, everywhere, and for anyone, to believe anything upon insufficient evidence," and so you suspend belief until evidence regarding the neighborliness of the new person comes in. What follows from this suspension of belief, is that you must treat the newcomer as neither a good nor a bad neighbor, you must be entirely neutral until the evidence is sufficient to settle the question. The way to do this would be to ignore her entirely.[3] We might even further suppose that you, being the inquisitive type, hire a private investigator to look into the background of the new neighbor to gather evidence of her character; he might conduct secret interviews with her past neighbors, check police records, and illegally tap her phone to help gather the data requisite to settling the question. This is of course an absurd way to proceed. But the absurdity of following the evidentialist in this case is not James's main point. Rather, James argues that in cases such as the one above, *suspending belief* is equivalent to adopting one of the hypotheses. To see this, recall that James's pragmatic conception of meaning says that when two seemingly distinct beliefs lead to the same action, they are in fact equivalent. Consider further that suspending belief about the neighborliness of the newcomer requires that you *ignore* her until sufficient evidence is in. But James's point is that *ignoring* a new neighbor is to treat her *as if* she were *not* a good neighbor. If suspending belief leads one to treat her as if she were not a good neighbor, it is equivalent to believing that she is not.

So, the second part of James's thesis has been established. The good neighbor example demonstrates that in certain genuine options, suspending belief comes to the same thing as adopting one of the hypotheses. Suspending belief about whether the new person is a good neighbor comes to the same thing as believing that she is *not* a good neighbor.

Hence we see the force of the first part of James's thesis. Under certain conditions, the evidentialist's rule of suspending belief when evidence is lacking is strictly *inapplicable*. That is, in a genuine option, we cannot fail to adopt one of the hypotheses, and when evidence is insufficient, something else not only *may* but *must* guide our decision.[4] James calls this "something else" our "passional nature." Although James is not as explicit as one would wish about what he means by "passional nature," we can glean from the essay that the term is meant to include not merely our momentary desires, but our more general wishes and hopes for the world. So, in the neighbor example, James would claim that if you are the kind of person who hopes for good neighbors, you are fully within the realm of epistemic responsibility to adopt the hypothesis that the new person *is* a good neighbor—and so to *treat* her as such—even if the evidence is lacking.

James pushes the point a bit further than this strictly logical objection to evidentialism. James contends that the evidentialist ethic of belief is not only inapplicable to certain cases but is moreover sometimes *irrational*. We can see this by considering James's characterization of the

On James

evidentialist position. According to James, since they believe that having no belief is better than having a false belief, evidentialists are governed by the commandment, "Shun Error!" (WWJ, 727). To this, James contrasts another possible intellectual directive, "Believe Truth!" Of course, the two principles are not mutually exclusive—by aiming to believe truth we also aim to shun error, and vice-versa. The question is rather one of the *prioritization* of the rules. The evidentialist places the epistemic command to shun error above all else; consequently, she would rather believe nothing than run the risk of adopting a falsehood. As James characterizes the position, the evidentialist advises, "believe nothing...keep your mind in suspense forever" where evidence is insufficient (WWJ, 727). By contrast, James confesses that he takes the command to believe truth to be primary; this means that he thinks "the risk of being in error is a very small matter when compared with the blessings of real knowledge" (WWJ, 727). Put another way, the evidentialist takes being a dupe to be the worst thing that could happen to a person, epistemically speaking, whereas James contends that "worse things than being duped may happen to a man in this world" (WWJ, 727). Unlike the evidentialist, James allows certain kinds of epistemic risks, where such risks are necessary for discovering the truth.

Now, to see that that the command to "Shun Error!" is irrational, briefly consider again our example. Recall once more that in suspending belief about whether our new neighbor is a good neighbor, you must pretty much ignore her. Yet by ignoring her, you actually *discourage* her from extending to you the common courtesies that go along with being a good neighbor, and so you actively *prevent* good-neighborliness from manifesting itself. *Suspending belief* is in practice *the same thing* as *not believing* that she is a good neighbor; and by not believing that she is a good neighbor, you help *make* her not neighborly, even if she is in fact a person who is generally friendly and courteous to her neighbors! Hence the evidentialist commandment to "Shun Error!" can actually *prevent* you from coming to know certain truths. What are we to say about an epistemic commandment that can *foil* our attempts to gain knowledge? James's response is clear:

> A rule of thinking which would absolutely prevent me from acknowledging certain kinds of truth if those kinds of truth were really there, would be an irrational rule. (WWJ, 733)

Faith and Risk

According to James, what the good neighbor case shows is that certain kinds of truth require *belief in advance of conclusive evidence.* To use his own example,

> *Do you like me or not?* ... Whether you do or do not depends, in countless instances, on whether I meet you half-way, am willing to assume that you must like me, and show you trust and expectation. The previous faith on my part in your liking's existence is in such cases what makes your liking come. (WWJ, 730).

Recall from our earlier discussion James's definition of faith as "the readiness to act in a cause the prosperous issue of which is not certified in advance" (WWJ, 333); in this sense, "faith is synonymous with working hypothesis" (WWJ, 336). Again, James reiterates that faith is like a kind of courage, a willingness to take certain kinds of risks for the sake of realizing some good. As we can see in the good neighbor example, James recommends that we take the *risk* of believing that the newcomer *is* a good neighbor in the *hope* that she will prove to be so. The Jamesian strategy is risky in that on some occasions our hopes will not be realized; the new person may prove to be a bad neighbor, and our initial efforts will in the end seem foolish. James's point, however, is that, insofar as neighborliness is an important good that *requires* an initial ungrounded faith in order to manifest, taking the risk of believing in the absence of evidence is warranted. In fact, he calls any intellectual maxim that would advise *against* such epistemic risk-taking "insane":

> There are cases where a fact cannot come at all unless a preliminary faith exists in its coming. *And where faith in a fact can help create the fact*, that would be an insane logic which should say that faith running ahead of scientific evidence is the 'lowest kind of immorality'[5] into which a thinking being can fall. (WWJ, 731)

One final point is in order before moving on. Although James rejects the evidentialist's categorical command to "Shun Error!," he does not abandon entirely the idea of evidence. Even in cases such as the good neighbor case, James holds that our belief should be responsive to evidence. The point is that in certain cases the necessary evidence *cannot come* until we invest our belief in the truth of the hypothesis. To return once more to our example, I *hope* that the person moving in next door will prove a good neighbor. Despite the fact that evidence is entirely lacking, I adopt the hypothesis on passional grounds that she is a good neighbor, and consequently I treat her *as* a good neighbor. James's argument is that *unless* I believe that the newcomer is a good neighbor, I cannot *discover* whether she is. Of course, as we said above, my efforts might prove futile and even foolish. It may turn out that, despite my neighborliness, the person next door is in fact a bad neighbor. This is certainly a question to be decided on evidence. The point is that this evidence could not come *prior* to my belief; I must make what is commonly, and fittingly, called a "good-faith" effort to be neighborly *before* the evidence can issue.

The Case for Religious Belief

What we have seen, by means of an extended examination of the good neighbor example, is that evidentialism is flawed in that it is not, as Clifford maintained, categorically applicable. What the analysis has shown is that when confronted with a genuine option, the evidentialist ethic of belief is (1) *impracticable*, in that suspension of belief is equivalent to adopting one of the hypotheses; and (2) *irrational* in that, even if it were practicable, it would foreclose the possibility of gaining certain kinds of knowledge. Hence James has completed the first stage of his argument.

What we have yet to see is how any of these considerations constitutes a defense of religious belief. That is, James has yet to argue that the option concerning religious belief is sufficiently like the good neighbor case so as to warrant a similar analysis. What James needs to demonstrate, then, is that the question of whether to adopt religious belief is a genuine option that cannot be settled on intellectual grounds. The recognition of this missing piece leads us into the second stage of James's argument.

The Religious Hypothesis

It is important to be clear at the outset about *exactly* what James means to defend under the name "religious belief," for James is no theologian. On James's view, the "religious hypothesis" consists in the conjunction of the following two propositions:

(1) The best things are the more eternal things.

86

(2) We are better off even now if we believe that the best things are the more eternal things. (WWJ, 731-732)

This may strike you as an odd characterization of religious belief since there is no specific *theology* contained in James's hypothesis. Religious belief, as James will defend it, is decidedly *not* fixed on traditional theological foci; the religious hypothesis does not include statements about the existence of God, the immortality of souls, eternal rewards and punishments, or the nature of evil.[6] As we mentioned in the previous two chapters, James believes that religion is "a living practical affair" (WWJ, 356) rather than a matter of intellectual abstractions and highfalutin doctrines. Accordingly, the religious hypothesis, as James construes it, should be understood as *recommending an attitude* towards the world rather than *making a claim* about what exists. As proposition (2) above suggests, the religious hypothesis is essentially a hypothesis about what it is best for us to believe. As we have seen, on James's view, *believing* is essentially tied to *acting*. Hence religion is for James an essentially *personal* matter, and the religious hypothesis is essentially addressed *to us*, to our lives here and now.

With the religious hypothesis spelled out, we can take advantage of some familiar terminology. Specifically, we may use the term "religious option" to name the option between accepting the religious hypothesis or accepting its denial. Given our preliminary distinctions in this chapter, identifying the religious option as such leads to the question: Is the religious option a *genuine* option? In other words, is the religious option *living, forced*, and *momentous*?

First, let us recall that whether the option is living in part depends upon the person to whom it is posed. There are some persons for whom the religious hypothesis is not live, and there are other persons for whom the denial of the religious hypothesis is not live; for both groups, the religious option is dead. Interestingly, James's argument is not addressed to either group; that is, James does not aim to convince those who are decidedly irreligious to adopt the religious hypothesis, and he does not attempt to give the religious believer further cause to believe. His target is rather the person for whom the religious option is living—the person who is "on the fence," and especially the person who *would* believe but does not due to lack of evidence.

Second, it should be clear that the religious option is a forced option. One must either adopt the hypothesis or go without it, and since believing is essentially tied to acting, one who suspends belief on the matter of the religious option is *pragmatically* in the same position as the one who positively *rejects* the religious hypothesis; both equally lose out on the truth of the religious hypothesis if it is true.

Finally, is the religious option momentous? James contends that it is, arguing that insofar as it proposes that "We are supposed to gain, even now, by our belief, and lose by our non-belief, a certain vital good" (WWJ, 732), we are confronted with a momentous choice. But what is the "vital good" that the religious hypothesis promises? Though James is not explicit here, we can surmise that this good cannot be otherworldly; it cannot be eternal rewards or ultimate salvation. The vital good offered by the religious hypothesis must take effect *now*, and the risk of loosing out on that vital good if we do not adopt the hypothesis is what makes the option momentous.

"Vital Questions" and Religious Commitment

The religious option, we believe, is intimately related—even equivalent—to what James calls elsewhere the "radical question of life," which is "the question whether this be at bottom a moral or unmoral universe" (WWJ, 341). In concluding our study of James, we hope to deepen our sense of the momentousness of the religious option through its connection to this vital question.

To begin, it is important to recall that this "radical question" is *not* a question of metaphysics as James understands it; that is, he is not asking the traditional philosopher's question of whether the properties of good and evil *really exist*, for as a radical empiricist, James is committed to the *reality* of moral experience. Rather, James's "radical question" is a question of the *future* of the universe, a future which is, according the pluralist, in part decided *by us*, by means of our actions and attitudes.

So, as James formulates it, the really "vital question" of life is, "What is this world going to be? What is life eventually to make of itself?" (WWJ, 404). In this way, the religious option is actually an option between two different *attitudes* towards the future of the universe. The religious hypothesis can then be seen as the hypothesis that,

> The highest good can be achieved only by our getting our proper life; and this can come about only by help of a moral energy born of the faith that in some way or other we shall succeed in getting it if we try pertinaciously enough. (WWJ, 340)

Religious Commitment

Conversely, the rejection of the religious hypothesis is then the hypothesis that our moral energies are not necessary to achieve the highest good.[7] James assures us that this is a forced option since "The universe will have no neutrals in these questions" (WTB, 109). Our actions will instantiate one or the other hypotheses in the option—we shall either take up the project of trying to better the world, or we will not. What shall we do?

If we take the evidentialist view and wait for evidence to decide the question for us, we fail to adopt the religious hypothesis and consequently fail to act on behalf of the world's improvement. For every moment in which we suspend belief on the matter, we forever lose an opportunity to help *make* the world a "moral universe." If we are resolute in our evidentialism, we put off indefinitely the salvation of the world; in the meantime, the world may further deteriorate or even end. In other words, by waiting for evidence, we may help to *make* the world an "unmoral" place. James punctuates this point by means of a set of analogies:

> If I refuse to stop a murder because I am in doubt whether it be not justifiable homicide, I am virtually abetting the crime. If I refuse to bale out a boat because I am in doubt whether my efforts will keep her afloat, I am really helping her to sink. If in the mountain precipice I doubt my right to risk a leap, I actively connive at my destruction. (WWJ, 344)

By contrast, the persons who adopt the religious hypothesis are able to say in response to James's "radical question": "This world *is* good...since it is what we make it,—and we shall make it good" (WWJ, 340). Of course, in adopting the religious hypothesis, they certainly violate the evidentialist command to "Shun Error!" Clearly they take a certain risk with their belief insofar as they commit to the project of making the world good without prior evidence to assure them that they can succeed. Consequently, the most earnest efforts to save the world may fail—it may be an unmoral universe after all. The point is that *we do not know* whether the universe is at bottom moral or not. The question of religious belief is then, on James's view, the question of whether we should act *as if* it were a moral universe or not. In other words, we can act as if it is moral, and if it is, then we shall help *make* the universe moral; but if it is not, we shall categorically fail to make the universe moral; and yet, our failure will be noble and courageous. On the other hand we need not act as if the universe is moral, and if it is not, we shall perish just like everyone else; however, if it *is* moral, we shall have actually *contributed* to the

On James

universe's demise by means of our inaction and cowardice—the universe's failure will be *our* failure.

We now can see that James's defense of religious belief is perhaps better characterized as a defense of religious *commitment*. The religious believer, on James's view, is not simply someone who holds certain beliefs about the existence of God and the afterlife. That is, religious belief is for James not belief *that* God exists or that hell awaits the wicked; it is rather belief *in* a certain moral project, a dedication to a certain cause, a resolution to engage in a certain long-run endeavor. In this sense, James's religion is a radically empirical meliorism, and the defense of religious belief is actually a defense of what we had called in the previous chapter the "moral life."

* * *

Capturing the essence of his own philosophical vision better than anything we could contrive, James concludes "The Will to Believe" with a passage from Fitz-James Stephen. We close our own discussion of James by reproducing this quotation in full.

> What do you think of yourself? What do you think of the world?... These are riddles of the Sphinx, and in some way or other we must deal with them.... In all important transactions of life we have to take a leap in the dark. If we decide to leave the riddles unanswered, that is a choice; if we waver in our answer, that too is a choice. But whatever choice we make, we make it at our peril. If a man chooses to turn his back altogether on God and the future, no one can prevent him; no one can show beyond reasonable doubt that he is mistaken. If a man thinks otherwise and acts as he thinks, I do not see that any one can prove that *he* is mistaken. Each man must act as he thinks best; and if he is wrong, so much the worse for him. We stand on a mountain pass in the midst of whirling snow and blinding mist, through which we get glimpses now and then of paths which may be deceptive. If we stand still we shall be frozen to death. If we take the wrong road we shall be dashed to pieces. We do not certainly know whether there is any right one. What must we do? Be strong and of a good courage. Act for the best, hope for the

best, and take what comes. If death ends all, we cannot meet death better. (WWJ, 734-735)

Endnotes

[1] Bertrand Russell, *The Will to Doubt* (New York: Philosophical Library, 1958), 38.

[2] Clifford, "The Ethics of Belief." *The Ethics of Belief and Other Essays* (Buffalo: Prometheus Books, 1999), 77.

[3] While it may not seem that "ignoring" is the appropriate "neutral" response, it is our contention that the practice of treating new persons *as if* they are neighborly (which is not morally neutral and like everything else, James would argue, cannot be an a priori duty) already undermines the evidentialist view. Such a practice of "neighborliness" is, thereby, a good example of what James is recommending with regard to faith more generally.

[4] It is worth emphasizing here that James intends this point to apply *only* to the genuine option that cannot be settled on evidence; in all other cases, James agrees with the evidentialist. James writes, "Let us agree, however, that wherever there is no forced option, the dispassionately judicial intellect, with no pet hypotheses, saving us, as it does, from dupery at any rate, ought to be our ideal" (WWJ, 729).

[5] James here is reiterating a quote from T. H. Huxley (1825-1895) he employed earlier in the essay (WWJ, 721).

[6] "That the God of systematic theology should exist or not exist is a matter of small practical moment" (WWJ, 357).

[7] Note that on this view the religious hypothesis is rejected both by those who deny that there is a highest good that could be realized (viz., pessimists) and by those who maintain that the realization of the highest good is inevitable (viz., optimists).

Selected Works for Further Reading

The secondary literature on William James is far too vast to allow for a comprehensive list of even the most important work. Keeping our audience in mind, we list below both James's own published work and only a selection of secondary material on James. Those wishing to pursue more detailed or focused study will find able guidance in many of these texts.

Original Works by William James

Original publisher and publication date (all of which are out of print) are listed followed by publisher and date of both selected editions still in print and the publisher (Harvard) and date of the critical edition.

Principles of Psychology, 2 vols. 1890. Holt. Republished by Dover (1950) and Harvard (1981; out of print).

Psychology (Briefer Course). 1892. Holt. Republished by Dover (2001), University of Notre Dame Press (1990), and Harvard (1984; out of print).

Will to Believe and Other Essays in Popular Philosophy. 1897. Longmans, Green, and Co. Republished by Dover (1956) and Harvard (1979; out of print).

Talks to Teachers on Psychology and to Students on Some of Life's Ideals. 1899. Holt. Republished by Longmans, Green, and Co. Republished by Dover (2001) and Harvard (1983; out of print).

Suggestions for Further Reading

The Varieties of Religious Experience. 1902. Longmans, Green, and Co. Republished by Dutton (1976), Penguin (1982), Random House (1993), Scribner (1997), and Harvard (1985; out of print).

Pragmatism: A New Name for Some Old Ways of Thinking. 1907. Longmans, Green, and Co. Republished by Dover (1995), Prometheus (1991), and Harvard (1978).

A Pluralistic Universe. 1909. Longmans, Green, and Co. Republished by Harvard (1977; out of print).

The Meaning of Truth: A Sequel to "Pragmatism". 1909. Longmans, Green, and Co. Republished by Prometheus (1997) and Harvard (1978).

Some Problems in Philosophy: A Beginning of an Introduction to Philosophy. 1911. Prepared for publication by H. M. Kallen. Longmans, Green, and Co. Republished by University of Nebraska Press (1996) and Harvard (1979; out of print).

Collected Works of William James

Essays in Radical Empiricism. 1911. Edited by R. B. Perry. Longmans, Green, and Co. Republished by University of Nebraska Press (1996) and Harvard (1976; out of print).

Essays in Pragmatism. 1970. Edited by Alburey Castell. The Free Press.

The Writings of William James: A Comprehensive Edition. 1977 [1967]. Edited by J. J. McDermott. University of Chicago Press.

Essays in Philosophy. 1978. Harvard. (out of print)

Essays in Religion and Morality. 1982. Harvard. (out of print)

Essays in Psychology. 1983. Harvard. (out of print)

Essays in Psychical Research. 1986. Harvard. (out of print)

Essays, Comments, and Reviews. 1987. Harvard. (out of print)

William James: Writings 1902-1910. 1988. Edited by Bruce Kuklick. Library of America.

William James: Writings 1878-1899. 1992. Edited by Gerald E. Myers. Library of America.

Correspondence of William James

The Correspondence of William James, 12 vols. 1992-2004. Edited by I. Skrupskelis and E. M. Berkeley. University Press of Virginia.

On James

Secondary Literature

Allen, Gay Wilson. 1967. *William James*. Viking.

Barzun, Jacques. 2002. *A Stroll with William James*. University of Chicago Press.

Coktin, George. 1989. *William James, Public Philosopher*. University of Illinois Press.

Cooper, Wesley. 2002. *The Unity of William James's Thought*. Vanderbilt University Press.

Cormier, Harvey. 2000. *The Truth is What Works: William James, Pragmatism, and the Seed of Death*. Rowman and Littlefield.

Feinstein, Howard. 1984. *Becoming William James*. Cornell University Press.

Gale, Richard. 1999. *The Divided Self of William James*. Cambridge University Press.

Gavin, William. 1992. *William James and the Reinstatement of the Vague*. Temple University Press.

Myers, Gerald. 2001. *William James: His Life and Thought*. Yale University Press.

Olin, Doris, ed. 1992. *William James's Pragmatism In Focus*. Routledge.

Oliver, Phil. 2001. *William James's "Springs of Delight": The Return to Life*. Vanderbilt University Press.

Perry, R. B. 1996. *The Thought and Character of William James* (abridged, 1-vol. version). Vanderbilt University Press.

Putnam, Ruth Anna, ed. 1997. *The Cambridge Companion to William James*. Cambridge University Press.

Seigfried, Charlene. 1990. *William James's Radical Reconstruction of Philosophy*. SUNY Press.

Simon, Linda. 1998. *Genuine Reality: A Life of William James*. Harcourt Brace.

Suckiel, Ellen K. 1984. *The Pragmatic Philosophy of William James*. University of Notre Dame Press.

Taylor, Eugene and Robert Wozniak, eds. 1996. *Pure Experience: The Responses to William James*. Thoemmes.